AYURVEDA COOKBOOK FOR BEGINNERS: VATA

A Sattvic Ayurvedic Cookbook Backed by Timeless Wisdom of Indian Heritage to Balance and Heal Your Vata Dosha!!

Rohit Sahu

Copyright © 2021 Rohit Sahu

All rights reserved. No part of this publication may be reproduced, distributed, or transmitted in any form or by any means, including photocopying, recording, or other electronic or mechanical methods, without the prior written permission of the publisher, except in the case of brief quotations embodied in critical reviews and certain other non-commercial uses permitted by copyright law. For permission requests, write to the publisher at the email below.

Published by: Rohit Sahu
Contact: rohit@rohitsahu.net
Published Worldwide

CONTENTS

Title Page
Copyright
Foreword   1
An Introduction to Ayurvedic Cooking   5
Benefits of Ayurvedic Cooking and Diet   12
Common Misconceptions in Ayurvedic Cooking   19
Rules to Consider for Ayurvedic Diet   28
An Introduction to Vata Dosha   39
Tastes That Pacify Vata   44
Setting Up an Ayurvedic Kitchen   52
Soups   61
Rice Dishes   74
Sabji (Cooked Vegetables)   88
Curries   102
Raitas   120
Chutneys   130
Sweets   141
Beverages   158
Indian Special   170
Food Combining for Doshas   194
Vata Seasonal Guide (Ritucharya)   198

Ayurvedic Diet FAQs	201
Author Note	205
Here's Your FREE GIFT!!	208
More from Author	210

FOREWORD

India is well-known for its classical medical systems, which include Ayurveda, Siddha, and Unani. Medical systems are listed in the Vedas and other ancient scriptures. Ayurveda, which derives from ancient Vedic scriptures, is a 5,000-year-old medical ideology and philosophy based on the idea that we are all made up of different types of energy.

Since the ancient Indian system of health care is based on perceptions of man and his health, the literal sense of Ayurveda is "Science of Life." It has been mentioned that good health requires having a well-balanced metabolic system.

The term is derived from the Sanskrit terms "Ayur" (Life) and "Veda" (Knowledge). Atharvaveda, which includes 114 hymns and incantations identified as miraculous remedies for diseases, also provides the roots of Ayurveda. There are numerous theories about the origins of Ayurveda, such as Dhanvantari (or Divodasa) receiving it from Brahma. Tradition also claims that the Ayurvedic texts were inspired by a lost text written by the sage Agnivesa.

Ayurveda is one of the few ancient medical systems that is still commonly studied in modern days due to its natural and easy approach.

It is regarded as a Sub-Veda or branch of wisdom dealing with physical well-being and prosperity on Earth and hence has considerable importance in human life. The Vedas (four books of knowledge) is the foundation of Vedic civilization, which dates back 40000 years. This is a sign of Ayurveda's ancient origins.

Ayurveda is also regarded as the "Science of Longevity" because it includes a systematic method for leading a long and stable life. It provides practices for body rejuvenation by diet and nutrition. It contains remedies for certain common illnesses, such as food allergies, for which there are few modern treatments. However, it should be noted that the Ayurvedic Diet is not a "magic pill" but demands the patient's complete cooperation to thrive. It is a user-friendly and practical immersive system. It helps the person to be self-sufficient and accountable for his/her health. Ayurveda is not a nutritional scheme for those looking for an escape or a reason to harm their bodies or mind anymore. It is a system of empowerment, prosperity, and long life.

It is believed to foster good health, natural beauty, and longevity. Despite its antiquity, Ayurveda is based on fundamental values and is a vibrant, rising body of wisdom that is as important today as it was in previous centuries.

This traditional form of Indian medicine was established by ancient sages whose sharp findings culminated in the creation of constitutional medicine. Traditional Chinese Medicine has a similar background.

Ancient physicians divided the cosmos into multiple forms of manifested energy and delegated the same energy to food and herbs. They viewed the cosmos as a continuous dance of energies, with an imbalance creating stress and disease in the body. It was the Vaidya's or physician's responsibility to control the body-mind environment.

The human body, according to Ayurveda, comprises tissues (Dhatus), waste (Malas), and biomaterials (Doshas). Plasma (Rasa), blood (Rakta), muscles (Mamsa), fat (Meda), bone (Asthi), marrow (Majja), and sperm are the 7 Dhatus (Shukra). Ayurveda, like classical antiquity's medicine, has traditionally classified bodily substances into 5 classical components, "Panchamahabhuta"—Earth, Water, Fire, Air, and Ether.

In addition, there are 20 Gunas (qualities or characteristics) that are thought to be innate in all matters. Heavy/light, cold/hot, unctuous/dry, dull/sharp, stable/mobile, soft/hard, non-slimy/slimy, smooth/coarse, minute/gross, and viscous/liquid are the 10 pairs.

According to Ayurvedic principles, health care is a highly individualized activity since everyone has a unique constitution, or Prakriti, that determines his or her physical, physiologic, and mental character, as well as disease vulnerability.

The three elemental bodily doshas are Vata (space or air, equated with the nervous system), Pitta (fire, equated with enzymes), and Kapha (water, equated with the digestive system) (earth and water, equated with mucus). Psychology is governed by a parallel set of mental doshas such as Satogun, Rajogun, and Tamogun.

Each dosha has unique characteristics and roles within the body and mind; the natural predominance of one or more doshas describes a person's physical constitution (Prakriti) and personality. According to Ayurvedic practice, a significant etiologic aspect of the illness is a mismatch between the bodily and mental doshas.

While all 3 doshas are present in everyone, Ayurveda suggests that we each have a dominant dosha that is unwavering from birth, and ideally an equal (though often fluctuating) balance between the other two.

If doshas are balanced, we are healthy; when they are unbalanced, we develop a disorder commonly expressed by skin problems, impaired nutrition, insomnia, irritability, and anxiety.

Vata, Pitta, and Kapha are all important to our biology in some way, so no one is greater than, or superior to, any other. Each has a very specific set of basic functions to perform in the body.

Although all 3 doshas are present everywhere in the body, the ancient Vedic texts describe a "Home Location" for each of the doshas.

"Vata is mainly found below the navel, Pitta mainly between navel and heart, and Kapha above the heart."

Each of the doshas has its own special strengths and weaknesses, and with a little awareness, you can do a lot to remain healthy and balanced. You can use this series to adjust your lifestyles and routines in a way that supports your constitution.

As per one Ayurvedic viewpoint, the doshas are balanced when they are equal to each other, while another viewpoint claims that each individual possesses a special combination of the doshas that characterize this person's disposition and characteristics. In either case, it states that each person can change their behavior or atmosphere to increase or decrease the doshas and preserve their natural state. Ayurvedic practitioners must find out an individual's bodily and mental dosha composition since such Prakriti is said to predispose one to specific diseases.

An individual who is slim, shy, excitable, has a prominent Adam's apple, and loves esoteric knowledge, for example, is most likely Vata Prakriti and hence more vulnerable to disorders such as flatulence, stuttering, and rheumatism. While the Ayurvedic text Charaka Samhita often relates "insanity" (Unmada) to cold food and abduction by the ghost of a sinful Brahman, deranged Vata is also correlated with such psychiatric illnesses induced by excited or excess Vayu (gas) (Brahmarakshasa).

Vata energy is correlated with air and space, and it is associated with bodily activity, such as breathing and blood circulation. Vata energy is said to predominate in people who are active, ambitious, and creative thinkers. When Vata is out of control, it may trigger joint pain, constipation, dry skin, anxiety, and other problems.

Pitta energy is linked with fire, and it is believed to govern the digestive and endocrine processes. People with Pitta energy are characterized as having a fiery temper, being intellectual, and being quick-witted. Ulcers, inflammation, digestive disorders, frustration, heartburn, and arthritis may occur when Pitta energy is out of control.

Kapha energy, which is associated with the chest, torso, and back, is related to earth and water and is thought to regulate growth and strength. Kapha types are assumed to be heavy and stable in constitution, and usually peaceful in nature. According to Ayurvedic practitioners, when Kapha energy is out of control, it may induce obesity, diabetes, sinus problems, insecurity, and gallbladder problems.

Ayurvedic teachings claim that stress, an unhealthy lifestyle, the atmosphere, and stressed relationships may all affect the equilibrium that occurs within a person's doshas. Individuals are more vulnerable to illness as a result of these unbalanced forces.

To align these energies, the concepts of proper lifestyles, eating behaviors, and daily and seasonal routines practiced in Ayurveda can be implemented with appropriate modification.

Ayurveda shows a high emphasis on food standards. According to Ayurvedic philosophies, food has a significant impact on an individual's physical, temperamental, and mental growth. Food is the essential building block for the development of the body and a life-sustaining critical matter known as Rasa. The Rasa is transformed into body components and aids in all aspects of life.

Food is the major source of dietary requirements, but with rising modernization, certain traditional practices are being discarded. As a result, modern eating practices affect balanced nutrition. There is an ever-widening nutritional deficit, and as a result, everyday life is no longer normal. However, the affluence of the working community, shifting lifestyles, and the decreasing affordability of medical treatment, both in terms of time and resources, are several of the factors that are currently pushing people to think about their health.

With this "Ayurveda Cookbook For Beginners Series," I provide you the best dietary practices, recipes, and everything you need to balance and heal your doshas alongside enjoying the authentic Indian flavors.

AN INTRODUCTION TO AYURVEDIC COOKING

Food is the fuel for the human body, for it to grow, live, and survive. An infant can grow to be a 150-pound individual because of food. The primary classification of food is focused on its suitability for the body and mental constitution, as determined by the 5 elements and the tridosha theories. In the natural transition of any material, living or non-living, 5 elements merge and dissociate.

Ayurveda is a 5000-year-old health-care system that believes science, philosophy, and spirituality are all essential components of living a healthy life. Ayurveda is more than just a medicinal system; it is often regarded as a way of life.

Living an Ayurvedic lifestyle is mostly about finding balance, and there are many ways to do so by cooking.

Food is referred to as "Ahara" in both Ayurveda and Yoga. According to Ayurveda, "Ahara" is one of the 3 key pillars of life, the other two being sleep and a well-regulated sexual life.

Ayurveda emphasizes Ahara (diet) and Anna (food) as a means to a decent life, fitness, and well-being, and asserts that proper nutrition nourishes the mind, body, and soul. Ayurveda does not classify food as good or bad; rather, it stresses different factors that affect food, such as its biological properties, origin, environmental factors, seasons, preparation, and freshness, and gives a logical description of how to balance food according to one's dosha and physical needs.

Ahara is derived from the Sanskrit root "Hru," which has a broad sense that includes the earth, water, heat or fire, air, and space; all 5 elements of this universe that sustain and support our existence.

Ayurveda teaches us how to maintain the body and its processes healthy to support Liberation. Yoga teaches us how to help the inner system, the spirit, and thereby indirectly support our liberation. As a result, Ayurveda and Yoga complement each other. The ideas of these two sciences have inspired Indian cooking. This is why it adds to the overall development of our well-being.

Humans exist in various parts of the world with unique climates, vegetation, ecosystems, and so on, and as a result, foods vary. Since certain basic foods are shared by all individuals, this traditional method of Indian cooking can be developed anywhere with minimal changes. Some vegetables, for example, have similar basic properties and can be interchanged.

Because of the complexity of recognizing the properties created in new combinations, creating new food combinations is a major task. Many traditional dishes in India have been developed and accepted by yogis since ancient times. New variations that are approved by experienced yogis may become a part of this culture. Carrot is an example of new food that has been cross-checked by yogis and is being added to Ayurvedic Cooking.

Another critical aspect of the impact of food on the system is an individual's Prakriti. An individual's Prakriti is described by a collection of physical, physiological, and psychological characteristics. For example, based on taste preference, individuals can be grouped as Vata (having an affinity for sweet, sour, and salty tastes); Pitta (with liking for sweet, bitter, and astringent taste), and Kapha (for pungent, bitter, and astringent tastes).

A meal should help our constitution's development as well as the overall health of our system. Each constitution has various traits, such as a proclivity for hard work, talkativeness, insomnia, or a tendency to think deeply. Food can help to sustain a person's natural instincts and constitution. Improper food consumption may put a burden on or damage some of an individual's natural activities.

The Ayurvedic Diet is an eating plan that determines where, how, and what to consume depending on your dosha, or body type.

Your dosha decides which foods you can consume to foster inner harmony, according to this diet.

Since everyone's digestive ability differs, eating the right food in the right amount is essential for living a balanced life. Food—when eaten in adequate amounts—offers vitality, vigor, healthy skin, and encourages tissue health.

The Pitta Dosha, for example, prefers cooling, energizing foods and avoids spices, nuts, and seeds.

Meanwhile, the Vata Dosha prefers wet, moist, grounding foods and avoids dried fruits, bitter herbs, and raw vegetables.

Lastly, the Kapha Dosha chooses fruits, vegetables, and legumes over heavier foods like nuts, seeds, and oils.

All 3 doshas must avoid red meat, artificial sweeteners, and processed foods. Instead, the Ayurvedic Diet recommends the consumption of natural whole foods.

Ayurvedic Diet is difficult to comprehend from a Western perspective, where the amount is measured by serving size, portion size, or caloric intake.

Compared to western dietary understanding and the US diet guide, Ayurveda says that a diet should be vegetarian (plant-based) and that portion size should be personalized for each person based on their needs, body constitution (dosha), and Agnibal (digestive power).

Since diet is the most significant factor in human health, many diseases can be avoided by consuming the right food at the right time, according to one's constitution or Prakriti.

Ayurveda believes that there is a subtle connection between disease manifestation and the 6 psychological expressions of lust, rage, envy, desire, attachment, and ego. These psychological states are integrally associated with foods. This relation is further discussed in terms of 3 states of being, namely Sattva, Rajas, and Tamas, each of which has distinct effects on the body and mind:

Sattva

Sattva guna denotes the mode of goodness. Sattvic food is light, pure, and high in prana (life force). It cleanses the body, calms the mind, and assists in the attainment of peace and equilibrium between body and mind. Sattvic food has been seen to increase Ojas in the body. It also assists in the repairing and creation of high-quality body tissues.

Rajas

Rajo Guna represents the mode of passion. Rajasic food is heavy, spicy, fatty, and sour. Rajasic diet includes non-vegetarian items such as seafood, chicken, and eggs, as well as beverages such as tea and coffee.

Tamas

Tamo Guna represents the mode of ignorance. Tamasic food is unhealthy and promotes traits such as lust, greed, and rage. Tamasic diet includes stale food, beef meat, and liquor.

Also, the quality and properties of food, such as heavy, light, and oily, should be considered. Rice, as compared to heavy and fatty pork meat, can be quickly digested. As a result, the quality and quantities of food are often weighed based on how well the food is digested.

Ayurveda stresses that a diet must be carefully chosen and wisely planned, not only based on a person's physical requirements and Prakriti but also taking into account the seasonal and everyday shifts and other natural factors that surround an individual.

According to Ayurveda, consuming wholesome food encourages wellness while eating unwholesome food induces disease. Food is classified according to their action on the individual and is defined by their specific qualities: Ras (taste), Virya (active component or potency), Vipak (post-digestive effect), and Prabhav (pharmacological effect).

As a result, food is classified based on its properties and its effect(s) on digestion. Since taste (Rasa) is important in digestion, food classification and food groups are formed based on taste.

Sweet (Madhura), Sour (Amla), Lavana (Salty), Pungent (Tikta), Bitter (Katu), and Astringent (Kasaya) are the 6 tastes (Rasa) of the food. These 6 tastes refer to the 6 phases of digestion. Each taste contributes significantly to the activation of the digestive and immune systems.

When various foods are combined and their properties are not complementary—indigestion, flatulence, and acidity may occur, as well as the formation of toxins in the body. However, when consumed separately, the same food can be easily digested and can stimulate "Agni."

Ayurveda believes every food is a medicine, so there is no such thing as bad or good food. It provides a clear approach to developing healthy foods for optimum health by formulating food groups that function in harmony, facilitate proper digestion, and encourage full absorption of vital nutrients.

Food that is similar to one's dosha aggravates the dosha. As a result, to balance the dosha, the appropriate food group must be picked. Ayurveda suggests:

a. Eat as little raw fruit and vegetables as possible.

b. Get prior knowledge of herbs and their effects before using them.

c. Avoid food combinations that are antagonistic, such as bananas with milk.

Ayurveda claims that the plants and plant goods we eat have a huge effect on our physical and mental well-being.

Ayurveda warns against consuming too many raw foods and limiting leftovers for good digestion. For proper nutrient assimilation, fresh, homemade food is suggested. Spices are used to make food more compatible and to counteract the harmful impact. Warm food activates Agni and digestive enzymes, so it is advisable to eat warm food. Food intake is often regarded for Vata people looking for smaller meals and eating more often. The best times to eat are at dawn and dusk. Pitta people should consume their largest meal at noon (a maximum of 3 times per day), while Kapha people should skip breakfast and eat their largest meal at lunch. Age and gender are also important considerations.

Elderly people should adopt an Anti-Vata diet, whereas middle-aged people should follow an Anti-Pitta diet, and children should follow an Anti-Kapha diet. Similarly, men should look for an Anti-Pitta diet while women an Anti-Kapha diet. It is best to have a calm and clear mind for optimum digestion. It is not advisable to eat when experiencing strong feelings such as tension, frustration, or sadness, as this may trigger an irregular and abnormal digestion process and harm the mind, which is the core for all sensory control and perceptions.

Herbs and spices are also essential in Ayurvedic nutrition since they help to add humoral balance to the food. For example, ginger neutralizes the heavy quality of the food, so adding ginger transforms the heavy food's property into a lighter state.

Similarly, when paired with various food agents, it adjusts its mode of action, such as ginger with rock salt reducing Vata symptoms, rock candy reducing Pitta, and honey reducing Kapha. Ginger is used to combating indigestion, flatulence, colic, vomit, stomach spasms, chest infections, cough, and asthma due to its versatility.

Herbs and spices, besides their healing properties, improve the taste and flavor of food and help in digestive secretions. Herbs and spices also include minerals and vitamins.

According to Ayurveda, the consistency of food ingested, food preparation, appearance, scent, and freshness of the food all have a strong effect on the mind. These elements influence all 5 senses and help to regulate digestion. Ayurveda promotes the selection of fresh food, preparing the food by mixing compatible foods, and the using of herbs and spices to improve the flavor and taste of the meal.

Thus, by blending foods for optimal nutrition and digestion and using spices and herbs in cooking to make the meal more digestible, Ayurvedic Cooking is a brilliant science of mixing ingredients and food items to preserve optimum health.

Ayurveda does not distinguish the method of cooking from that of digestion and nutrition. Ayurveda incorporates the study of nutrition and digestion with the science of cooking and puts a strong focus on digestion and nutrient assimilation. Proper recipe blends, food selections, food timings, and preparation techniques are all highly stressed.

That is why Ayurveda always advises to feed in a particular order. The emphasis is on easier absorption and the body's capacity to absorb the nutritious essence of the food eaten. The bulk of health issues are caused by an unhealthy diet. Furthermore, the food we eat should be seasonal and regional. Food, according to Ayurveda, plays an important role in well-being and survival.

Unlike our bodily constitution, which is impossible to alter, our mental mindset is highly affected by the food we intake on a daily basis, enabling us to choose between awareness, agitation, or inertia. We do so by choosing the correct foods; eating right is one of the keys to good health!

Ayurvedic Cooking techniques provide us with guidance on what to eat and how to eat to help the healing process and assist the body in removing contaminants and maintaining equilibrium. It contains a wealth of knowledge on healthy diet, proper food combinations, food quality, food timing, and cooking methods. As a result, diet is considered medicine in Ayurveda.

The norms of Ayurvedic Cooking may be daunting at first, but there are basic ways to align our diet with its principles. Ayurvedic Cooking is based on direct knowledge, but the methods of preparation are simple; you do not need to be a professional chef.

Cooking with fresh, high-quality, and organic ingredients is key. Ayurveda stresses the usage of seasonal and preferably regional foods. This method of eating fresh food encourages optimal wellness, removes contaminants, and maintains equilibrium if there is an imbalance. Ayurvedic Cooking enhances natural flavors while optimizing digestion, nutrient absorption, and waste elimination.

To boost taste and quality, food should be cooked and eaten as soon as possible after purchase.

For Ayurvedic Cooking, you just need to keep a few things in mind:

- Cultivate a relaxed, content, and optimistic outlook.
- Cooking should be enjoyable, arouse excitement, and taste delicious—it should not be limiting or devoid of flavor.
- Food should offer us pleasure and reconnect us with our bodies.
- Make the appropriate combination.
- Food should be both tasty and high in nutrients.
- Maintain personal hygiene (clean hands, hair tied, nails trimmed).
- Give spices the priority since they tend to balance the food.
- To reach dosha equilibrium, combine 6 tastes: sweet, sour, salty, bitter, pungent, and astringent.
- Use Sattvic ingredients to increase Tejas (intelligence), Ojas (aliveness and health), and Prana (life force).

All the recipes in this cookbook are traditional, time-tested over decades, and are focused on Ayurvedic principles. They are beneficial to human well-being when used properly. They can aid a yogic practitioner's yoga practice by keeping the mind relaxed and calm and are thus ideal for all yoga practitioners. The beauty of these recipes is that they are not only Sattvic in nature but are also tasty and have an authentic Indian taste!

While cooking is an art that should be learned under the supervision of a professional to ensure tasty and perfect outcomes, a few recipes can be learned by trial and error. I hope these recipes offer simple instructions and that you enjoy both cooking and eating.

BENEFITS OF AYURVEDIC COOKING AND DIET

Ayurvedic Cooking is well-known for its thorough natural healing methods that treat diseases and improve the human body and mind's overall health. The Ayurvedic Diet has been followed by millions of people for thousands of years and is widely recognized as a means of promoting physical health and wellness in many parts of the world.

Ayurvedic foods are appetizing, flavorful, and aromatic, and they are a way of offering love that transforms into healing when consumed in a stimulating setting. The elimination of toxins from the system and the body's electrochemical enrichment are the primary goals of Ayurvedic Cooking. It is therefore both an art and a science when cooking becomes alchemy and food becomes Tantra.

The advantages of Ayurvedic Cooking include enhanced health and wellness, increased stamina, freedom from anxiety and depression, greater emotion regulation, and feeling more at peace with oneself.

If weight loss is your goal, an Ayurvedic Diet focused on whole, unprocessed foods and mindful eating habits are likely to yield results.

Thus, the Ayurvedic Cooking and diet have many advantages and remedies for people of all ages, including the young, the elderly, the sick, the healthy, and anyone in between. Here are some advantages of integrating Ayurvedic Cooking and diet into one's lifestyle:

1. It Promotes the Consumption of Organic, Seasonal, and Locally Grown Foods

Since we need various sources of nourishment at different times of the year, the Ayurvedic Diet often shifts with the seasons. What one's dosha is, it's critical to eat a diet that balances whichever dosha is peaking due to the season. Kapha is said to peak in the late winter and early spring, Pitta in the summer, and Vata in the fall and early winter.

Here are some recommendations for adopting an Ayurvedic Diet depending on the season, according to Ayurvedic principles:

Winter: You may find a boost in your appetite and thirst because of the need to achieve inner warmth. Consume less cold and light ingredients, such as raw vegetables, smoothies, and salads. Consume more nourishing healthy fats and complex carbohydrates such as cooked grains, soups, and stews. Increase your consumption of sweet, sour, and salty flavored foods while decreasing your intake of sour, pungent, and bitter foods. To improve immunity, consume ghee, warming spices, and raw honey.

Spring: Eat more bitter, astringent, and pungent foods in the spring instead of sweet, sour, and salty foods. Lighter, drier, and warmer foods should be prioritized over heavy, fatty foods. Reduce your consumption of meat and fruits, raise your consumption of green vegetables, use warming spices, eat smaller servings, and increase your physical activity.

Summer: Consume more naturally sweet foods and fewer hot tastes (spicy, pungent, sour, salty) and dry foods (those that are astringent and bitter). Eat more cool, moist foods over dry foods; eat less fat and eat lighter foods. Reduce your intake of hot foods, soups, and stews, and increase your intake of fresh fruits and vegetables. More freshly produced juices, coconut goods, yogurt, smoothies, and cooling plants such as cucumber, berries, and melons are essential.

Fall: Eat sweet, mildly bitter, and astringent foods in the fall instead of pungent, sour, salty foods. Find a perfect balance for cooling and hot foods, as well as light and heavy foods. Consume more soups, warming spices, pomegranates, and well-ripened seasonal fruits. Consume more bitter, green vegetables and spices.

2. Helps with Weight Loss

A healthy diet and lifestyle changes based on Ayurveda will help you lose excess body fat. Weight is not a major issue in Ayurveda, but dietary patterns are. It is possible to achieve a toned body by empowering the body to detox through proper dietary restrictions.

Since the Ayurvedic Diet emphasizes nutrient-dense whole grains, it can help in weight loss.

It's uncertain if the weight reduction from the Ayurvedic Diet is due to dosha-based nutrition or the focus on healthy grains and mindful eating. However, some study has found that it is beneficial when paired with movement, such as Yoga.

One research, for example, showed that adopting an Ayurvedic Diet suitable for each participant's dosha promoted weight loss or good weight maintenance in 200 participants with a combination of the 3 doshas.

At the start of the study, Kapha and Pitta people were heavier than Vata people; but, after 2–3 months, the Vata community lost the most weight, while both the Pitta and Kapha groups increased in multiple aspects. According to the researchers, diets focused on Ayurvedic constitution may prove helpful in promoting weight loss.

Another small research discovered that adhering to an Ayurvedic-based lifestyle that involved eating adjustments and yoga sessions resulted in an overall weight loss of 13 pounds (6 kg) over 9 months.

Ayurvedic Diets have also been shown to help normalize hormones, increase insulin sensitivity, and prevent diabetes.

3. Aids in the Improvement of Mood

Ayurveda suggests that psychological factors such as lust, rage, greed, desire, attachment, and ego are inextricably related to food. Since the Ayurvedic Diet considers a person's individual body and mental type, physiological cycles and biological patterns, as well as seasonal changes and life stages, it can help boost mood stabilization and energy by tailoring the diet to their particular needs.

If anyone is anxious, having difficulty sleeping, or dealing with anxiety, an Ayurvedic Diet might provide more grounding foods like complex carbs and healthy fats. To suppress anger and lust, lighter foods such as smoothies and fruit are advised. Specific tastes, such as sweet, sour, bitter, and salty, are also used to counteract the harmful influences of a person's constitution.

4. Helps in Digestion

Many wholesome foods that are readily digested, nutrient-dense, and capable of enhancing gut health are included in Ayurvedic Diets. Traditional Ayurvedic practices, such as fermenting and cooking foods to make their nutrients simpler to digest, are used to alter the way wholesome foods are digested. Foods can be served raw, dried, smoked, fried, pickled, preserved, or steamed to help ease digestive pain.

There is proof that the Ayurvedic Diet can help people treat gastrointestinal disorders including hyperacidity, irritable bowel syndrome, hemorrhoids, diarrhea, constipation, and heartburn.

Another big advantage of adopting an Ayurvedic Diet is that it restricts refined, inflammatory foods, which may contribute to bad gut/microbiota health. Artificial flavoring, processed grains, and refined fats are examples of such foods. The Ayurvedic Diet places a strong emphasis on reducing "incompatibilities," or foods that are not well tolerated. Incompatibilities that can cause such items to be eliminated from a person's diet are determined by variables such as the food's processing, quantity/dose, time/season, the combination of ingredients, and personal tastes.

5. Reduces Inflammation

Inflammation may be caused by a poor diet, improper dietary habits, inadequate sleep, erratic sleep patterns, and poor digestion. Inflammation is the underlying cause of many illnesses, including brain disorders, cancer, asthma, cardiovascular problems, lung diseases, arthritis, and others.

The digestive system improves when you eat according to your dosha type. Toxins in the blood and digestive tract are reduced as these foods are consumed at the right times which reduces inflammation. As a result, you'll have more stamina, control, and a significant decline in lethargy and mood fluctuations.

Ayurvedic food is also well-known for its cancer-prevention properties. A mixture of turmeric and black pepper is the closest example of an herbal Ayurvedic formulation.

6. Lowers Blood Pressure, Cholesterol, and Illness and Disease Symptoms

Researchers believe that combining Ayurvedic Diets with relaxation techniques will help minimize plaque buildup. Plaque is caused by the accumulation of cholesterol and fats in the artery's inner lining. This is known as atherosclerosis and it is the underlying cause of heart problems and strokes.

Ayurvedic Diets include a variety of herbs, vitamins, nutrients, and proteins. These are combined with an adequate dose and given at the appropriate time to avoid and cure immune-related disorders.

Ayurvedic herbs and essential oils tend to enhance oxygen supply, improve blood circulation, and remove contaminants from the body via the skin.

7. Skin and Hair becomes Healthy

Do you want your hair to be smooth and shiny? With Ayurveda, you can avoid costly clinical procedures by opting for herbal and natural methods to produce a glow without wasting too much money. A nutritious Ayurvedic meal customized to one's Prakriti is adequate to support good skin and hair.

Ayurvedic general dietary recommendations emphasize the intake of fresh food while taking your dosha type, medical background, regional produce, norms, and traditions into account.

The focus is on foods rich in antioxidants, herbs, teas, vegetables, protein, and good fats.

8. Purifies the Body

Cumin, cardamom, fennel, and ginger are Ayurvedic herbal ingredients that relieve indigestion and avoid bloating. Through delivering these elements to the human body, food and toxins that interact with efficient bodily processes are eliminated. A cleansed body, in turn, leads to better overall health.

9. Promotes Well-Being

The Ayurvedic way of life promotes body-mind health through food, exercise, and proper sleep. Though Ayurvedic medicine has been studied for thousands of years, most of the data supporting its efficacy are focused on observation. However, as a curiosity in integrative approaches to health (like Ayurveda) grows, more scholars are performing high-quality studies that affirm the system's use in providing new insights into nutrition sciences.

10. Promotes Long-Term Good Habits

As you incorporate Ayurvedic Cooking and Diet in your lifestyle and see improvements, you're motivated to adopt other beneficial practices in your routine like yoga, pranayama, meditation, and other Ayurvedic practices that can boost your well-being further.

Harvard researchers published a report that supports the utilization of healthy living approaches such as Ayurveda to help people adhere to fresh, healthier habits over time.

11. Helps in the Battle Against Exhaustion and Lack of Immunity

An Ayurvedic Diet may also assist with exhaustion, lethargy, and tolerance to illnesses caused by stress. Cooked vegetables, buttermilk, and spices (garlic, cardamom, pepper, and ginger, and honey) are all used to raise vitality, avoid anemia, and boost immunity. The Ayurvedic method involves herbs and nutrients, such as adaptogen herbs like ashwagandha and ginseng, besides a balanced diet, to boost the body's capacity to cope with stress.

12. Encourages Mindfulness

Aside from the foods you consume, mindfulness is an essential aspect of the Ayurvedic Diet.

Ayurvedic traditions call for mindful and intuitive eating. This involves paying attention to your food as well as your body's cues towards it. It involves taking the time to appreciate your meal, consuming when you're hungry, and stopping when you're finished.

Mindfulness is a practice in which you pay particular attention to how you feel in the present moment. Mindful eating stresses avoiding disturbances during meals to concentrate on the texture, taste, and smell of your food.

One small study of 10 participants found that cultivating mindful eating decreased bodyweight, depression, fatigue, and binge eating.

Mindful eating can also improve self-control and foster a positive eating pattern.

13. You Begin to Rely on Whole Grains

Some Ayurvedic practitioners advise their students to consume only foods grown locally. Although this is impossible for certain people, it will encourage you to consume more whole, unprocessed foods, which are generally healthier than refined foods.

While there are specific rules for each dosha in the Ayurvedic Diet, the diet as a whole recommends consuming whole foods such as fruits, vegetables, grains, and legumes. Since these foods are abundant in vital nutrients, they will significantly improve your well-being.

The diet also limits processed foods, which often lack fiber and essential vitamins and minerals.

As per research, consuming more packaged foods can increase the risk of heart disease, cancer, and even death. As a result, the Ayurvedic Diet can aid in the prevention of chronic disease and promote wellness.

14. Provides Generalized Nutrition

The Ayurvedic Diet does not exclude any specific food category. Instead, it includes a range of foods to favor and avoid depending on your dosha. As a result, it can provide nutritious food as you make healthy food choices.

15. Is Adaptable and Long-Lasting

The Ayurvedic Diet does not include strict obedience to the rules; participants will act independently on what works better for them and their bodies. If implementing the dosha food plan sounds too difficult or restricting, some experts recommend merely adhering to the core eating principles.

16. It Improves the Quality of Life

Ayurveda is a way of life that, when fully implemented, brings a surge of general well-being into your everyday life. With healthy dietary guidelines, efficient sleep schedules, home remedies, everyday and seasonal rituals, yoga, and pranayamas, Ayurveda will help you reclaim your fitness.

COMMON MISCONCEPTIONS IN AYURVEDIC COOKING

In any field, it is simple to accumulate urban-myth type knowledge, and Ayurveda is no exception. There are several myths around Ayurvedic Cooking. Below mentioned are a few food myths that have been debunked by Ayurveda:

1. Ghee, which is Widely Used in Ayurveda, is Inappropriate

Although due to the heavy nature of Kapha, ghee should be consumed in limit for them, but for cooking oils, Ayurveda clearly supports ghee. Fat is classified into two types: good fat (monounsaturated and polyunsaturated fats) and bad fat (trans fats). Ghee, which is commonly used in Ayurveda, is abundant in healthy fatty acids, which have miraculous benefits while not inducing weight gain. Weight loss, a healthy heart, glowing skin, increased energy are some of the benefits.

2. Grazing and Small Meals throughout the Day are Ideal for Digestion

As per Ayurveda, you should only consume your daily scheduled meals, which may be 2-4 times each day, or when you are genuinely hungry. If we continuously bring stuff in, nothing gets completely digested, and we end up with "Ama," or undigested food, in our system. Ama clogs channels and triggers several diseases.

If a snack is needed, it should be eaten at least 2 hours after the meal. Eat something light and easy to digest so that it is removed from the body by the time the next meal arrives. Few "emergency snack suggestions" (by dosha) are:

Vata: Spiced rice porridge, baked spiced apples with ghee and raisins, bread (banana, zucchini, or date bread), avocado or guacamole, miso soup

Pitta: Fresh fruit, vegetable sticks, soaked and peeled almonds, homemade coconut cookies

Kapha: Kale chips, dried fruit, popcorn, rice cakes, and baked spiced apples with cloves.

Snacking after dinner is the most harmful to digestive health. You can't sleep with a massive load in your stomach. But if you want to get something in your bloodstream after dinner, spiced hot milk is a good right-before-bed treat. It can be spiced with turmeric and ghee or cinnamon, cardamom, and nutmeg.

3. Smoothies Make Excellent Food Substitutes

Smoothies are undeniably easy to execute, delicious, convenient to carry when traveling, and packed with nutrients. This is unlikely with Ayurveda, and if you adopt an Ayurvedic Diet, you must know the drawbacks of smoothies.

Smoothies are typically made of raw foods that are hard to digest and have plenty of food for parasites. This promotes the growth of yeasts, microbes, and other parasites in your gut.

They are usually produced by mixing foods that, according to Ayurveda, should not be consumed together, such as fruits and vegetables, and chilled fruits combined with milk or yogurt. They can induce weakness, nausea, lethargy, and cold sensitivity.

The mixture of several ingredients in cold milk or frozen yogurt makes it tough to ingest when drunk by people who have a poor digestive fire. As a result, people with poor digestion should stop drinking smoothies.

Some examples of incompatible smoothies include:

• Fruit and anything is incompatible.

• Milk and bananas/sour grapes or melon are incompatible.

• Yogurt and milk are not compatible.

• Nightshades and yogurt/milk/melon/cucumber are incompatible.

4. It is Okay to Use Canned or Frozen Foods

Frozen and canned foods are popular, but Ayurveda does not prescribe them. According to Ayurveda, while frozen or canned foods are fast and simple to prepare, they contain preservatives and flavors that are detrimental to health when consumed daily. If you can't get fresh produce, it may be because it's out of season, which negates the good seasonal effects on doshas.

These processed foods can often include less desirable ingredients such as preservatives, sugars, and "natural flavors," all of which you do not want to consume.

They make our bodies feel inactive and raise inertia because they lack nutrition and taste. Foods are best eaten fresh and freshly prepared at home, according to Ayurveda. Organic, whole foods make up the perfect diet.

5. Tea and Coffee are Excellent Refreshments

Caffeine, which is used in tea and coffee, may have negative effects on the human body. While these drinks are deemed relaxing, drinking them in large amounts can increase the system's imbalance. Caffeine influences each Prakriti (body type/constitution) differently:

Vata Dosha: It increases nausea, panic, and nervousness, as well as jitteriness, shakiness, dizziness, and muscle tremors, as well as bloating, constipation, weak bones, and headaches.

Pitta Dosha: Caffeine can boost blood pressure for up to 2-3 hours after consumption in Pitta Dosha. It often causes irritability, frustration, headaches, indignation, short temper, and shortness of breath. Excessive intake may cause a sore stomach, nausea, vomiting, hyperacidity, heartburn, and gastric ulcers.

Kapha Dosha: It affects the kidneys and bladder. It slows digestion and stimulates urination.

6. Consume as Much Water as Possible

We are all mindful of the effects of consuming enough water, but no one focuses on what defines enough.

Although it is necessary to drink enough water, guzzling large quantities, particularly near mealtime, can extinguish the digestive fire. Fire is hot and dry, while water is cold and wet.

Water makes up 60% of our bodies, so consuming a lot of water will quickly result in weight gain, dilute body fluids, and weaken digestion. When our bodies want anything, it asks for it, and the same is true for water. As a result, we must only consume water when we are thirsty.

But there's also a huge percentage of people who do not consume enough water. Their bodies would then become conditioned to a low dosage of water. Then you must investigate other signs of dehydration, such as dry eyes, dry mouth, constipation, dark urine, and so on. If you have any of these signs, you must consume water even if you are not thirsty. Otherwise, just drink water while you are thirsty.

To live a healthier life, one should stick to a few basic water guidelines developed by Ayurveda.

1. Water quality should be monitored since consuming contaminated water will contribute to severe illnesses.

2. Instead of standing, drink water while seated. It aids digestion and ensures that you do not feel bloated after drinking water. Drink water in little sips.

3. Stop consuming water right before or after meals. A 40-minute gap is recommended to allow for easy digestion of the meal.

4. Stop drinking ice water because it can induce indigestion. You can take lukewarm water.

5. Pay attention to the body. If your lips are parched, your body needs water; similarly, if the color of your urine is yellow, your body is dehydrated.

6. Make it a routine to drink water first thing in the morning to help flush away toxins.

7. Nothing Complements Food more than Ice Water

The intestinal fire is killed by using ice water. To aid digestion, it is best to drink warm or at least normal water with meals. Ideally, the stomach should be half full of carbohydrates, a quarter full of water, and a quarter empty. It's best to avoid drinking anything for an hour before or during a meal. However, sipping ginger tea before a meal can help with digestion as ginger's warming effects improve digestive strength.

8. You Must Cook All the Time

Of necessity, cooking is good because there is less packaged food and you have power over the resources and ingredients that go into your food. However, healthy eating is a way of life, and you must begin where you are. The journey towards being more mindful of food, even though just by not consuming "low-fat" groceries, is a major improvement. One should not overthink, but seek local growers, cook most days, eat more organic, fast once a week, and avoid packaged or processed foods.

It's fine not to begin there. Every step is crucial. In restaurants, you can also pick the energetics of your meal. At the very least, offer the body the qualities it deserves (warm, moist, nourishing, easy to digest). At that moment, not forcing yourself to cook can even be a soothing choice. So, you can still live an Ayurvedic food lifestyle without having to prepare all the time.

9. Don't Waste Food; There are People Starving

This is something that every human is taught as a child. Although I wholeheartedly believe that food should not be wasted, consuming when you are not hungry is not the solution. In fact, when it comes to adapting to their bodies' needs, children outperform adults. If you have lavished your kid with candy and gifts, all bets are off. However, children will recognize that they are full, and they will not be hungry whether they have constipation (a clog in the digestive system) or have already consumed too much.

As adults, we need to be more mindful of our digestive system too. When we go out to dinner, there should be no shame in not completing a large plate of food, no matter how delicious it is. We must exercise self-control so that we do not overindulge. Limiting distractions when eating will help us become more conscious of our bodies and understand when we are full. Any leftover curry can then be saved for another day or given to the family pets.

10. Ayurveda is All about Indian Spices and Foods

Ayurveda does not necessitate or endorse any specific food or region. It's a pure wisdom to learn the energetics of food. Every meal has special properties, and you learn to pay attention to how foods feel in your mouth and stomach. Whatever you consume has its own range of energetics. Until you get comfortable sensing the energetics of food—with some education of course—you can apply that to any cuisine.

11. Carbohydrates are not Included in a Healthy Diet

We need carbohydrates besides proteins, vitamins, and healthy fat.

Have you ever asked how our forefathers stayed healthy despite eating too many grains? I accept that our culture has changed dramatically, and except for a few people, our lives are no longer as physically demanding. Carbohydrates, on the other side, aren't all that bad!

Carbohydrates provide energy. As a result, you must monitor your carbohydrate intake to your calorie expenditure. We don't need as many carbohydrates as most of us don't burn as many calories as our ancestors did. However, this does not imply eliminating all high-carbohydrate foods such as grains and potatoes!

Grains are very important in Ayurveda. Most grains are deemed sweet, which is the flavor used as a tonic in Ayurveda. We use our tissues and energies every day to conduct tasks. These must be replenished so that we do not deplete them.

Grains are the best source of nutrition. If there is an imbalance, there are grains for each dosha. However, for balanced people, any whole grain is a good choice! If you want to eat something light and easy to digest, begin with basmati rice. Some grains can be heavier and harder to process into nutrients, so a strong digestive fire is needed to "digest" them.

Many people are sensitive to overly processed grains, such as wheat, which has been genetically modified. To cover itself, the body speeds up the digestive tract to get grains out of it! I suggest exploring various whole grains. There are gluten-free grains available. Amaranth, buckwheat, rice, quinoa, and sorghum are all good options.

Grains such as rice, wheat, barley, quinoa, and many others render your diet more wholesome and nutritious, as well as helping to fill the needed portion of your stomach. The involvement of grains aids digestion, encourages satiety, and nourishes the body and mind, all of which are important for good health. Satiety is necessary for remaining grounded, reducing anxiety and exhaustion, and handling stress.

Furthermore, grains produce several amino acids (specific proteins), minerals, and other nutrients that are difficult to obtain from other foods.

Try to use 3 different grains for all 3 meals of the day for the best outcomes, just limit the grains to a minimum (half a cup would be ideal for a medium-built individual). Use potatoes and other carb-rich vegetables wisely, along with other fibrous vegetables. Use whole grains instead of fried grains. Take care not to overuse yeast with grains (which most of the bread has).

12. Fat should not be Included in Our Diet

After all, Ayurveda is all about ghee and carbs. It's difficult to move from the comfort of salad and low-carb living into the ecosystem of "consuming all foods." As per Ayurveda, not all fats are bad; in fact, some can help with weight loss.

We must know that our brain is largely composed of fat. The kidney is covered in fat, fat wraps around abdominal organs, and fat lubricates joints. Fat is necessary for the health of the skin, joints, gut, nervous system, and mind.

Thankfully, there has been much progress in disproving this myth, and we are becoming more aware of the benefits of good fat. 10% of our diet should be fat (remember, we don't have to get the 10% from oils because vegetables, proteins, and grains do contain varying amounts of fat).

However, be aware that the usage of certain types of fat can quickly boost blood fat levels and increase the likelihood of cardiac diseases, stroke, and other health issues. Have a small amount of good fat in your diet regularly.

Ghee, nuts, seeds, dairy (except butter), rice, and so on are all good sources of fat. However, remember to use these ingredients in moderation and to minimize fried foods and visible fat in proteins.

13. There are Different Diets in Ayurveda

Ayurveda not only tells us what to consume, but also when to eat, how to eat, and how much to eat.

We are always evolving, and our nutritional strategy should evolve with us. Food requirements vary in the winter versus the summer, in the morning versus the evening, at periods of high demand versus ease, at different activity levels, and during different moon phases or hormone cycles.

Ayurveda teaches you how to listen to what the body is asking for in real-time. This is accomplished by discovering appetite habits, digestive signs, bowel movements, and tongue observations. This will seem complicated, but it is not! If you've figured out how to decipher the secrets of the gut, you'll be able to help determine what diet will be a good match at the time. This becomes less of an analytical process and more of an intuitive one with time.

Ayurveda is more concerned about the "diet for today" than it is with a set of rules like Paleo or Veganism. So, don't buy the old Ayurvedic fallacy of eating in a certain way.

14. Traditional Indian Cuisine is TOO OLD for Today's Lifestyle

Traditional Indian foods have been prepared for several years, and preparation styles differ from region to region. Because of including functional foods such as body-healing ingredients, vitamins, dietary fiber, and probiotics, Indian traditional foods are often known as functional foods.

These functional foods aid in weight loss, blood sugar control, and support the immune system. Production techniques such as sprouting, malting, and fermentation improve the functional properties of foods much more.

15. You Must Eat at Regular Intervals

No, not really. We must only feed while we are hungry. And though we are all aware of this fact, there has recently been a trend—supported by several articles and guidance—that we should eat 3-5 small meals at regular intervals even though we are not hungry.

It is true that if our bodies are healthy and our metabolism is fine, we can feel hungry at regular intervals. However, it will differ based on our last meal, how we spent the day, and/or stress.

Essentially, appetite indicates that our body is ready to receive food.

So, if you are not hungry, wait until your body secretes the required digestive juices and you feel hungry so that your body can better absorb the food. Much of the time, an accumulation of undigested food is the root cause of a lack of appetite. As a result, driving more food would exacerbate the problem and could eventually lead to disease.

You would feel much healthier if you wait until you are hungry (which is actually a short fast). It will not be difficult for you to wait until you are hungry.

However, if you just have flashes of hunger, that may be due to bad digestion and a shortage of digestive juices. In such a case, when you wait for a proper appetite, you get exhausted. And much of the time, even after a long wait, you do not get a strong appetite. If you notice flashes of hunger, even though they are low, it is best to consume a small amount of nutritious food.

Remember, if the appetite isn't strong or consistent, seek help right away, since this is one of the first signs of a digestive disorder.

16. Salads are Always Healthy

Salads are generally healthy, although not always. When your metabolism is slow or your stomach is gassy, the body processes cooked or steamed vegetables more easily than raw salads. Bad digestive signs include a lack of appetite, exhaustion, bloating, and stomach pain. Salads are not a suitable choice for dinner, even if you have a moderate digestion, since our digestion normally slows down after the sunsets. And if you have digestive issues, you should also be cautious with salad dressings.

17. Ayurveda don't Emphasize on Seasonal Shifts

We adjust our foods and routines in Ayurveda to accommodate the season. In the autumn, we add oil and root ourselves; in the spring, we dry out and lighten up; in the summer, we relax. And what about winter? Early winter is Vata season, and it is still cold, windy, and dry. Late winter is Kapha, cold, wet, and heavy...

About seasonality, what we have to do is believe that nature is watching out for us. Seasonal foods aim to have the qualities required to avoid imbalances throughout each season. In the summer, cooling, sweeter foods, such as watermelon, are produced to relieve Pitta and heat. Late winter/early spring yields light, bitter greens that tend to break up the heaviness and congestion of Kapha. Squashes and heavy foods to ground and warm Vata are produced in the fall/early winter. Nature's wisdom to provide for its beings is a delight to live with!

RULES TO CONSIDER FOR AYURVEDIC DIET

We are all aware that eating nutritious foods is important for good health. What to eat is important, but so is knowing where to eat, how to eat it, and when to eat it.

The ancient Ayurvedic guidelines can help you stay healthy not only by the food you consume but also by how you eat it. Plus, it teaches us how to enjoy the meals and be grateful for the foods we eat along the way.

The following rules will help you tap into the ancient knowledge of Ayurveda and use it to achieve health, prosperity, and strength through food.

1. Choose Foods Based on Your Dosha Type

A person's doshic imbalance, classified as "Vikruti," is a mixture of two physiologic components that are heightened. Harmony with the body may be maintained by consuming foods that reduce the heightened components. The Ayurvedic guidelines mentioned below may be used to identify and prepare foods for the 3 doshas:

The **Vata Dosha** (Air and Space elements) is cool, dry, light, and rough by nature. Eating products that have the reverse impact provides equilibrium. Excess Vata energy can be balanced by foods that are warm (both in temperature and spice), hydrating (such as soups and stews), high in healthy fats (such as olive oil, ghee, organic cream, and avocados), and grounding (think dense, healthy comfort foods).

The **Pitta Dosha** (Fire and Water elements) is characterized by hot, oily, light, and sharp qualities. As a result, consuming foods that are cool (particularly in terms of internal cooling, as seen with peppermint, cucumber, cilantro, and parsley), astringent (beans, legumes, pomegranate, and green tea), moderate, and mild can help to reduce Pitta aggravation.

The **Kapha Dosha** (Earth and Water elements) manifests as heavy, cool, oily, and smooth. Eating foods that are light, warm, dry (like beans and popcorn), and rough (think "roughage" like vegetables) can easily cause Kapha balance.

2. Eat until You are Satisfied, Not Full!

We are all special, with varying stomach sizes and metabolic rates. We also have different dosha constitutions in Ayurveda, which govern how our bodies digest food. Aside from the apparent weight gain effect, overeating raises free radical growth in the body, which accelerates the aging process.

So, listen to your body and eat only to the point where you are satisfied. Never consume over two-thirds of that sum. A third of the stomach should remain empty to allow for proper digestion.

By throwing down your fork when you are satisfied but not stuffed, you stop overeating and your body gets the nourishment it deserves without the extra pressure of digesting and, in most cases, accumulating excessive calories.

3. Limit the Number of Ice-Cold Foods and Beverages You Consume

Agni, or the internal fire, is the digestive power of the physical and energetic body. Agni resembles a roaring campfire. It is ideal when it is hot, bright, and capable of digesting food, thoughts, emotions, and experiences. To stoke one's inner fire, avoid ice-cold foods and beverages that dull Agni's strength. If a constant stream of cold food or beverages is consumed, the Agni of all doshas will become exhausted. Vata and Kapha types can choose warm foods and teas, while Pitta types should appreciate cold (but not frozen) beverages and foods. Through this approach, intestinal power will be retained.

4. Enjoy Herbal Teas in between Meals

Tea is more than just a delicious beverage; it is also a potent healer that can help restore health, strength, and joy. To stop diluting Agni, drinks like teas should be drunk in moderation (no more than ½ cup) with meals. Teas, on the other side, maybe consumed liberally between meals and serve as herbal remedies. Drinking tea during meals provides the body with "liquid medication," decreases snack cravings, helps detoxification, and stokes the digestive fire.

Hot, spicy teas with cinnamon, ginger, and cloves can ground and calm Vata Dosha. Pittas, who may drink their tea hot or cool, can find cooling herbs like peppermint, coriander, and rose balancing. With licorice, black pepper, and cardamom, Kaphas can improve their vitality, digestion, and optimism.

5. Get the Largest Meal of the Day for Lunch

Agni is most intense when the sun is at its peak. Through having the biggest meal of the day at noon, the body will utilize its strong inner fire to break down and assimilate nutrients with less energy output than at other periods of the day. The midday meal is the perfect time of day to incorporate heavy or more difficult-to-digest foods. This is also the best time to splurge on food (think an icy drink or sugary treat). Through consuming the biggest meal at lunch, the body is well filled with energy throughout the day, helping to relieve the "afternoon energy slump."

6. Only Eat After Your Previous Meal has been Digested

According to the guidelines, you should not feed within 3 hours of your previous meal or snack, but you should also not go without eating for over 6 hours.

7. Eat High-Quality Food

Foods that are too dry or too oily should be avoided. Prioritize cooked vegetables, grains, and a small quantity of dairy.

8. Eat with All Your Senses

Use all 5 senses—Take time to enjoy the aroma of your meal, the appearance of your plate, the texture of your food, the many tastes, and the sounds you make when eating.

Color, scent, taste, and touch can all be appealing to motivate you to eat better. As a result, the digestive juices have a beneficial effect. The utensils must also be clean and appealing.

9. Don't Eat Too Fast

Chewing is an essential part of digestion and should not be rushed. Ayurveda highlights the significance of proper food chewing (50% of the digestion takes place in the mouth). One should chew the food not too quickly, but also not too slowly. It is vital to chew properly and moisten the food with saliva to help digestion, so do not overfill the mouth with food.

As a result, the juices produced are fully absorbed by the body. It also prevents overeating and chewing the food correctly makes us feel satiated.

So, take your time eating your food, don't just swallow it after one bite!

10. Eat at Regular Intervals

Nature, like our bodies, appreciates patterns and regularity. Also, eating on time improves overall well-being.

Eat a nourishing breakfast first thing in the morning; your big course of the day at high noon, when the sun (and your digestive fire) is at its peak; and a lighter dinner before sunset, before Agni fades.

As mealtime approaches, the body releases a decent number of digestive juices. One-third of the stomach should be left empty to enable the digestive juices to better combine with the food to balance the dosha. If you consume your meals and snacks too close together, your Agni (digestive fire) would be overworked, resulting in gas, bloating, and other types of indigestion.

Even if you have a hectic schedule, remember to set out a specific time for meals every day. And no nighttime snacking—you'll regret it in the morning!

11. Food should be Hot

Food should always be served hot and fresh. This promotes a healthy digestive system and helps to stabilize Vata. A balanced digestive system ensures the equilibrium of all body functions.

Since raw foods may be challenging to digest, it is safer that your meals are freshly prepared and consumed hot. To sustain the digestive capacity (Agni), Ayurveda suggests avoiding food that comes directly from the refrigerator. This helps the digestive enzymes to work properly.

12. Food should be Moist and Oily

Dry foods, such as sandwiches and dry roasted meals, are very difficult for the digestive system to process; instead, incorporate warm, moist foods into your everyday diet.

13. Drop Your Snacking Habits

Following a meal, 3 phases of digestion must be completed, according to Ayurvedic guidelines. The Kapha energies are powerful in the first hour after a meal. The body can feel bloated, sluggish, and sleepy. Pitta elements govern digestion two to four hours after a meal. During this time, hydrochloric acid levels increase, internal heat increases, and the meal is turned into essential nutrients for the body. Vata energies rise four to five hours after a meal. During this time, lightness and space return, and appetite rises.

Incomplete digestion happens as the digestive cycle is interrupted by more food. Incomplete digestion results in the buildup of Ama or contaminants over time, which may appear as a range of mild to severe symptoms. As a result, Ayurveda suggests eating three meals per day, with no treats in between, to maintain digestion and keep the stomach stress-free.

14. The Food should be Compatible and should have All 6 Tastes

Ayurveda recognizes 6 tastes, each of which expresses the physiology of a particular mixture of energy and information. The body receives a bio-diverse energetic palate by adding each of the 6 tastes into every meal. This energetic palate sends instructions to the body's cells that are specific to one of the taste groups.

Sweet, Sour, Salty, Bitter, Pungent, and Astringent are the 6 tastes defined by the Ayurvedic Diet.

Each taste has a distinct energetic influence on the mind and body. They either aggravate or calm specific doshas. Consider the Ayurvedic philosophy that "like increases like." Eating hot, spicy foods can add fuel to the fire for someone with Pitta excess.

You can easily balance the doshas and sustain your Prakriti if you schedule your diet according to your body type and its impact on each individual dosha.

The tastes may either help or hurt the doshas. A diet rich in sweet, sour, and salty taste, for example, alleviates or eliminates Vata Dosha. While a diet with astringent, bitter, or pungent taste will irritate Vata.

Pitta is often exacerbated by a pungent, sour, and salty taste. A sweet, sour, and salty taste aggravate Kapha.

The 6 tastes supply the following cellular details to the body:

Sweet: Grounding, strengthening, and nourishing

Sour: Purifying and cleansing

Salty: Balancing and regulating

Bitter: Detoxifying and mineralizing

Astringent: Anti-inflammatory and cooling

Pungent: Energizing and warming

You can integrate a tiny amount of each taste into each meal. It may be as little as a pinch of salt, a squeeze of lemon, or a slice of pepper, but as long as the taste is there, the energetic equation is complete.

15. Keep an Eye on Your Health Conditions

There are also disease-specific or medicine-specific guidelines for food intake that must be met.

Cough patients should eat vegetables like coccinea, spices like garlic, cardamom, long pepper, and ginger, and condiments made of puffed rice.

It is said in the Charaka Samhita Vimana Sthana to consume food in the proper quantity that is warm and unctuous.

16. Only Eat When You are Hungry

We assume we are hungry at times, but it is more probable that we are dehydrated. Allow at least 3 hours between meals and pay attention to the signs the body is sending you.

As the juices from earlier food intake settle down, the energy levels drop somewhat, signaling the body's hunger quotient.

17. Eat in a Relaxed and Pleasant Environment

The environment in which one eats is also important; it should be clean, appealing, peaceful, and, if possible, secluded. Ayurveda discourages standing when feeding, so sit down and enjoy your meal calmly and comfortably.

Eat in a friendly, quiet atmosphere, free of loud noise, music, TV, radio, or other disturbances, in a relaxed seating position on the floor or in a chair.

This will allow you to focus on your diet and how it makes you feel, enabling you to savor every bite and eat gradually and mindfully.

18. Ayurveda Advises against Eating while Wearing Shoes

The heat produced thus disturbs the digestive system, which is why Ayurveda suggests washing one's feet and sitting cross-legged.

19. Avoid Disturbances When Eating

How many times have you eaten while reading a novel, watching TV, reviewing emails, or answering phone calls? According to the Ayurvedic Diet, mealtime is an occasion to interact with the intrinsic energies and wisdom of the food you eat. See the colors, experience the spices, and raise awareness of the sunshine, soil, and earth that have come together to produce the energy wraps that are food.

If you're new to eating with deep awareness, start by eating just one meal a day in silence and concentrating on each of your senses for a few minutes at a time.

20. Stop Eating Three Hours before Going to Bed

During sleep, the body cleans, cures, and recovers itself, whilst the subconscious digests the day's thoughts, emotions, and memories. The physical healing and mental digestive mechanisms are halted as the body's energy is diverted towards physical digestion. To prevent this imbalance, Ayurveda advises that the last meal of the day be light and completed three hours before bed. As a result, the body's prana is free to rest and repair at the deepest depths during sleep.

21. Consider Wholesome Food

It is important to prepare nutritious food while doing Ayurvedic Cooking. According to the ancient sage Charaka, nutritious food is the source of well-being and joy. Unhealthy eating is to blame for suffering and illness.

Eating healthily encourages healthy mental well-being (Sattva), enthusiasm, and energy (Urja).

Such foods and liquids, when consumed properly, nourish the body tissues (Dhatus), increase strength and immunity (Bala), enhance the complexion of the skin (Varna), and soothe the sense organs.

Improper food intake harms both body and mind.

Food wholesomeness is influenced by the amount (Matra) of food eaten, the period of consumption (Kala), the preparation of food (Kriya), the habitat of the food grown (Bhumi), the body type of the individual consuming the food (Deha Prakriti), and the dosha imbalance of the person.

22. Take Small Bites

A tiny bite should be chewed thoroughly, causing it to blend well with Saliva and speed up the digestion process. It is a good dining etiquette.

23. Chew the Food Thoroughly

According to Ayurveda, how you eat is more important than what you eat. One of the golden eating laws of Ayurveda is to chew every bite of food 32 times. (That's the first phase of the digestive process, so one should do it properly!) Chewing well helps you to eat more slowly and mindfully which avoids overeating.

24. The Mind should be Calm while Eating

Thank God or your mom, wife, or sister, and visualize your heart filling with love and goodness. That will create the perfect atmosphere for the body to profit the most from it.

25. Give Importance to Food Processing

Food is graded in Ayurveda depending on its type and purpose.

Grains, pulses, refined foods, milk goods, leafy vegetables, fruits, salts, supplements, various forms of water, oils, and alcoholic beverages have all been produced and defined based on their biological impact.

They are also categorized depending on their sources and seasonal variations.

Food processing is a subject that is discussed in detail. The pharmacological properties of a substance may be changed by the cooking process. As opposed to flaked or cooked rice, which is heavy to digest, puffed rice is light on the system.

26. Avoid Eating while You are Stressed, Angry, or Grieving

When you are tense or emotionally triggered, the nervous system goes into fight-or-flight mode rather than rest-and-digest mode. As a result, the body will have a more stressful time digesting food. Instead, do a calming activity during that stressful period and feed afterward, once you're calm.

27. Ayurveda Supports a Fully Vegetarian Diet

That implies no beef, fish, seafood, eggs, and mushrooms. But it does support the consumption of milk and milk products obtained from the cow without violence. When consumed appropriately, cow's milk and milk goods are very beneficial.

28. Eat Whole, Fresh Foods

Prana, or the life force, nourishes the body at the most basic level and handles the production of vitality, strength, and energy. Food's many components, such as vitamin, mineral, and phytonutrient content, are simply reflections of the energetic, or Pranic, imprint.

The easiest way to increase Ojas, the supplier of life energy in the body, according to the Ayurvedic Diet, is to increase Prana. Foods rich in Prana come directly from the Earth. Their Prana was created by combining the energies of light, water, and earth. The moment food is picked, its Prana starts to wane. As a result, consuming foods as close to their harvest period as possible would raise Prana more readily than eating the same foods further away from harvest time. Local community support agriculture and farmer's markets are invaluable opportunities for locating fresh, high-life-force foods.

29. Consume Seasonal and Local Ingredients

What's growing in your area is the healthiest food for your gut. Fresh foods that have been sun-ripened produce more Prana than foods that have been imported and stored thousands of miles from their harvest, according to Ayurvedic guidelines.

30. Go for a Walk after Each Meal

The traditional Ayurvedic ritual of walking for at least 15-20 minutes after a meal assists in the flow of food into the gut. According to one report of diabetic patients, it can even lower blood sugar levels after eating.

32. Avoid Incompatible Foods

Another distinguishing characteristic of Ayurvedic Cooking is its understanding of food content and processing incompatibilities.

According to Ayurveda, there are 18 kinds of incompatibilities.

Incompatibilities occur when the efficacy of the food—processing, quantity, ingestion phase, duration, or season are inconsistent or have a negative effect on each other. In Ayurvedic Cooking, mixing foods like sour fruits and milk or honey and ghee in the same amounts is a No-No.

Milk is deemed incompatible with horse gram, fruit, or fish. Even heating honey is discouraged. While I do not have a modern scientific explanation for these laws, they can be explained in Ayurvedic terminology as incompatible due to the nature of the foods themselves.

The processing of an item will alter its efficacy, safety, and pharmacological impact.

In most dosha imbalanced cases, yogurt is deemed unwholesome. There are basic guidelines for consuming yogurt. It should be consumed alongside food items that balance its adverse effect.

When unwholesome yogurt is churned and the butter is removed, it becomes a healthy drink.

In Ayurveda, this sweet-tasting yogurt beverage is known as buttermilk. It's recognized as "Takra" in Hinduism. After two days in an earthen vessel, it produces an astringent taste and becomes a nutritious meal for the gastrointestinal tract.

It's particularly helpful for hyperacidity, irritable bowel syndrome, fissures, hemorrhoids, and some cases of diarrhea and dysentery.

Some Other Mindful Food Habits to Practice Include:

• Before you begin eating, give thanks or sit in silence for a minute.

• A couple of sips of warm water during the meal will aid digestion but avoid drinking too much of it.

• After you finish eating, sit calmly for a few minutes before going on to the next task of the day. Because when you rush to the next activity soon after eating, the body gets a shock as it was busy secreting digestive juices and you stood up suddenly. Give it a few minutes to know that you've finished eating.

AN INTRODUCTION TO VATA DOSHA

Vata is represented by the elements air and ether (space). Like autumn air, the quality of Vata is cool, light, dry, subtle, windy, mobile, sharp, moving, hard, rugged, and clear. The balanced nature of the Vata feels happy, excited, cheerful, and strong. Signs of Vata deficiency are an overactive brain, anxiety, feeling cold and dry, tiredness, fatigue, nausea, gas, bloating, and constipation.

Nourishing Elements: Fire, Water, and Earth

Nourishing Attributes: Moist, Heavy, Smooth, and Warm

Nourishing Tastes: Sweet, Salty, and Sour

Essential Minerals: Calcium, Copper, Iron, Magnesium, and Zinc

Macronutrients: Carbohydrates 50-60%, Protein 30%, Fats 15-20%

Functions of Vata: Create Energy, Endocrine Gland Function, Elimination, and helps to Distribute Nutrients at a Cellular Level.

Locations: Bladder, Colon, Thighs, Feet, Lumbar Region, and in the Skin.

Foods Beneficial to Vata: Most Nuts, Fruits, Cooked Vegetables, and Cultured Dairy Products.

Food to Avoid: Broccoli, Cauliflower, Dry Grains, and Peas

Exercise Beneficial to Vata: Yoga, Walking, and Slower Exercise for a Minimum of 30 Minutes a Day.

Vata is the invisible force of movement that controls all movements—breathing, blinking, contraction of muscle and tissue, pulsation of the heart, and all movements of the cytoplasm and cell membranes—and coordination across the mind and the nervous system.

Vata encourages innovation, creativity, and versatility in a balanced way. But it also causes fear and anxiety when out of control.

Vata provides the basic motion for all body processes and is extremely important for well-being. On an annual basis, Vata is most common in the fall and seasonal shifts, and these are the most important times to be cautious of diet and lifestyle.

One aim of lifestyle considerations is to regulate this motion. Routine is very useful in helping the Vata to efficiently ground all of this moving energy.

A person with a prevailing Vata is blessed with a quick mind, versatility, creativity, and imagination. Mentally, they usually understand ideas easily, but then forget about them just as quickly. Ready, energetic, and very productive, Vata people walk, talk, and think very quickly, but they are easily exhausted.

They seem to have less willpower, courage, boldness, and capacity for fluctuation than other types and often feel insecure and unsubstantiated.

Vata types may become afraid, nervous, and anxious when unbalanced. Vata types have differing appetites and digestion. They are often drawn to astringent foods such as salads and raw vegetables, but their composition is balanced by warm cooked foods and sweet, sour, and salty tastes. Their feces are often stiff, dried, and low in size and volume with a propensity to contain a little urine.

Vata resides in the stomach, as well as in the head, ears, bones, joints, skin, and thighs. Vata people are more susceptible to infectious illnesses such as emphysema, pneumonia, and arthritis.

Certain common Vata disorders include flatulence, tics, twitches, aching joints, dry skin and hair, nervous disorders, constipation, and mental confusion. Vata tends to increase with age in the body as shown by the drying and wrinkling of the skin.

In Ayurveda, the Vata Dosha is the lightest and most innovative of all doshas. When they are out of control, their creative minds and bodies, which are always on their way, will overwhelm themselves with fear and chaos.

Vata is the most mobile of the doshas, and although it's quick to get out of control, it's also simple to regain.

One of the most important ways to support Vata is by setting up a daily routine and following a Vata-balancing diet. By encouraging both, we make it possible for our bodies to work in harmony at all times.

In Balance

When in balance, Vata personalities are energetic, vibrant, joyful, polite, open-minded, free in spirit, embrace change and learn quickly, are clear and aware, sleep long and comfortable, have a proper appetite, healthy circulation, and even body temperature.

We perceive people with dominant Vata as enthusiasts, light, and imaginative. They're quick-witted and open to new opportunities. In fact, they're involved and like to move. We like their comfort and easiness, but not their forgetfulness.

Vata people are in love with music and dance. They can relax well when listening to classical music, enjoy warm and gentle oil massages and forget about themselves and the world in the process. A warm environment and comfortable materials such as silk, silk-wool blend, and cotton on the skin provide a simple inner balance; the rooms in which they stay will radiate warmth and comfort. A comfortable chair or couch with a cozy fleece blanket makes them relaxed easily.

Spontaneity often leads people with a Vata constitution to reckless, worthless money spending. If, on the other hand, Vata people live in harmony, they remain lively, polite, and creative beings for their entire lives. They are closely linked to the spiritual, which is why meditation is simple for them as long as they take the time to do so.

When Vata is in equilibrium with their secular existence, they are coordinated in body and mind and their response to stimulation.

When they're in equilibrium, Vata helps them to handle their emotions, feelings, thoughts, and behaviors effortlessly. Their ambulation is simple, their sensory integration and their mental processes float, and they feel expansive, imaginative, and energized.

If their Vata is in equilibrium, their breathing strengthens their nervous system, and there is homeostasis between tissues and organs. The flow of their Prana is controlled by the Vata, and this feature helps them to inhale quickly and to yield (exhale) with ease as well.

Out of Balance

When a Vata person is out of balance, he or she may be exhausted or stressed, forgetful or distracted, restless, and frizzy with a lack of focus. They can have difficulty falling asleep, experiencing occasional constipation, and poor circulation.

When the Vata is out of control, there is a propensity for unnecessary activity and agitation within the body and mind. This can lead to anxiety, exhaustion, insomnia, and panic. In the physical body, Vata deficiency is expressed as coldness, dryness, and constipation. In the skin, the excess can be seen and perceived as raw, rugged, flat, fine lines, premature aging, and wrinkles.

While some of Vata's characteristics sound like imbalances, such as dryness or disruption of sleep, possessing a Vata-dominant nature is not necessarily an imbalance. All the doshas have certain characteristics that we can try to match through the rules of Ayurveda. Learning one's constitution is the secret to deciding which of these principles is the most relevant.

Anyone can develop Vata imbalances, but Vata-dominant people are more likely to experience Vata imbalances.

What Causes Vata Dosha or Imbalance?

Ayurveda's basic tenet is "like increases like." As a result, increasing the inherent qualities of the (dry, light, cold, rugged, delicate, and mobile) would increase the Vata in your body. You may also experience pain when the Vata is out of control. So what causes the Vata imbalance?

Cool is not cool: Dry/cold weather conditions can increase your body's Vata imbalance. So if you're a Vata type, stay hot!

Dry/Cool Foods: Avoid pungent or bitter food. Dry and cold food can also make the Vata worse.

Bored to Vata: Dry thoughts, cold behavior will make the Vata worse.

A few other factors include:

• Stress

• Grief

• Traveling

• Irregular schedules

• Late-night activity

• Childbirth

- Surgery
- Excessive exercise
- A dry, rough, and/or raw diet

TASTES THAT PACIFY VATA

One of the basic teachings of the Ayurvedic tradition is that everything in the universe consists of 5 elements—earth, water, fire, air, and ether (space). The tastes are no different; each of them contains all 5 elements. That said, each taste is made up of 2 elements.

The 6 Tastes and Their Predominant Elements

Sweet (Madhura)	Earth and Water
Sour (Amla)	Earth and Fire
Salty (Lavana)	Water and Fire
Pungent (Katu)	Fire and Air
Bitter (Tikta)	Air and Ether
Astringent (Kashaya)	Air and Earth

How Tastes Influence Doshas

Balancing the Doshas

The 6 tastes help balance our doshas with what we're consuming. Sweet taste, for example, creates earthy Kapha, cools hot Pitta, and reduces airy Vata. Because it is a nourishing taste, it increases the volume of all tissues. Therefore, we live off sweet-tasting foods, such as oats, root vegetables, and rice, because they keep us healthy and strong.

Temperature

Each flavor affects the body's temperature, either by heating it up or cooling it down. Of starters, cinnamon is pungent and warm, which increases body temperatures. Grapes are sweet and cooling, which can help you cool down.

Quality (heavy or light, wet or dry, penetrating or soft)

Taste defines the quality of whether food is light or heavy to digest, or wet or dry on mucous membranes. Black pepper is spicy, light, dry, and penetrating—easy to digest, dries mucous membranes, and penetrates deeply into the tissues. Chew on the peppercorn, and these characteristics will be obvious to you!

Direction (where the food goes in the body)

Remarkably, the tastes have an affinity to certain parts of the body. Like garlic goes to our lungs as we can smell it. Ginger has multiple 'sites,' clearing mucus from the lungs, heating the skin, stimulating the blood, and relaxing the muscles. Asparagus is known for having the smell of urine—Ayurveda says asparagus is a bitter, cooling food that releases internal heat through the urinary system.

It's no accident that we use some of the 6 flavors to define emotional experiences or patterns quite explicitly. We equate to love, kindness, and caring nature with sweetness. They have a mutual understanding of what a salty individual's personality could look like, and most of us can see someone who has become particularly bitter over the years.

Since Vata itself is delicate, it appears to respond very well when we make positive changes to the energies that surround us. When it comes to balancing your Vata Dosha, there are several important reminders about the flavor of your life, relationships, and memories.

In fact, connections and experiences that are filled with sugar are profoundly pacifying for the Vata. It may be an indulgent massage, taking some time to be completely present with a sweet baby or a loved one, a romantic evening with your partner, a nourishing chat with a close friend, or a loving self-care practice that you do regularly. There are many ways to do this, but intentionally seeking a little extra sweetness in our day-to-day experience can support Vata at a very deep level.

Vata types are often attracted to friends and loved ones who are the salt of the earth—people who are firmly rooted, consistent, trustworthy, and stable. Such qualities are used to counterbalance Vata's remote, simple, and transparent qualities.

Vata may also benefit from being around a salty character that exudes courage, confidence, or sustained enthusiasm because these qualities counteract the tendency of Vata towards anxiety, fear, and boredom. If you don't have a friend or a relative who embodies these characteristics, simply focusing on cultivating courage in yourself can be very helpful.

On the other hand, dry humor, dry experiences, and bitterness tend to worsen the Vata in general. These would include any part of your life that makes you feel isolated, separate, cynical, or bored because they have the potential to raise your Vata's cold and dry nature.

Remember, Ayurveda sees taste—from the most tangible sensory experience to the most subtle energetic influence—as an essential therapeutic tool. While each of the 6 tastes has a vital role to play, the perfect combination of tastes can vary wildly from person to person.

When it comes to balancing Vata, the sweet, sour, and salty tastes tend to be the most supportive, while too much of the pungent, bitter, and astringent tastes can certainly be aggravating.

Pungent, bitter, and astringent tastes increase Vata and all phenomena related to the movement, penetration, and purification of channels. Therefore, if you need to pacify Vata, you need to focus on sweet, sour, and salty tastes, and eat more warm foods.

So to Balance Vata:

Emphasize:

Sweet

-It is mainly composed of earth and water elements and is heavy, oily, moisturizing, soft, grounding, nourishing, and building.

-It has a mild laxative effect and can help to counter Vata's tendency towards constipation.

-Its antispasmodic nature helps to soothe twitches, tremors, and other neuromuscular Vata imbalances.

-It nourishes all the tissues of the body and is both replenishing and rejuvenating.

-Activates downward flowing force in the body, which is calming and stabilizing the Vata.

-It has an attraction of mucous membranes and can help prevent the dry, rough effects of Vata on these tissues.

-Promote naturally sweet foods such as bananas, most grains, root vegetables, milk, ghee, fresh yogurt, nuts, beans, and oils.

-The sweet taste is the basis of a Vata-pacifying diet. It is the predominant taste in most Vata staple foods and also the primary source of nutrition for Vata.

-Emphasizing the sweet taste does NOT require us to eat large amounts of refined sugar or yummy-sweet foods. In fact, doing so tends to exacerbate the tendency of the Vata to over-exert and then crash. Naturally, sweet food tends to be grounding, nourishing, power-building, and satisfying.

Precaution:

The sweet taste should be minimized when excess mucus, excess weight, excess fat, and excess sleep are present—imbalances that are not typically associated with Vata but may still be present in people with Vata constitutions or imbalances.

Sour

-It is mainly composed of earth and fire elements that make it liquid, oily, moist, and hot.

-It has an affinity to most tissues in the body and helps to build up the bulk of the tissue.

-It is digestive and promotes appetite, overall metabolism, proper elimination, and also specifically helps to eliminate gas.

-It has a unique ability to clear up the dryness and expel the excess Vata.

-Promotes appreciation, understanding, discrimination, and understanding—mental attributes that support Vata.

-It awakens the mind and helps to unite scattered energy.

-It's downward moving energy grounds Vata.

-Support sour additives such as lemon juice or lime juice, a dash of vinegar, a side of kimchi or sauerkraut, a bowl of miso, a slice of cheese, or a dollop of sour cream.

-Sour fruits such as green grapes, oranges, pineapples, and grapefruit are also suitable when consumed separately from other foods and in moderation. These are great Vata-pacifying snacks.

-In general, the taste of sour is not the centerpiece of a meal; instead, it tends to enhance and enliven other flavors.

-Sour taste stimulates the mind and the senses, improves digestion, promotes energy, moisturizes other foods, and helps to eliminate excess wind (gas and bloating).

Precaution:

In cases of congestion, excess heat, itching, skin conditions, and imbalances in the blood, sour taste should be minimized. While these discomforts are not usually associated with Vata, they may still be present in people with Vata constitutions or imbalances. The sour taste is also best minimized when the weather is extremely hot and humid.

Salty

-It is mainly composed of elements of water and fire that make it heavy, oily, moist, and warm.

-Aids the appetite, metabolism, absorption, assimilation, elimination, and is also anti-flatulent.

-It nourishes and promotes growth, muscle strength, and flexibility.

-It helps to cultivate courage and respect and can therefore counter Vata's tendency to fear.

-It is antispasmodic and has an affinity for the nervous system, where many Vata imbalances occur.

-It moisturizes the body and helps maintain the balance of the electrolyte water, which is easily disrupted by excess Vata.

-Its energy moves downwards and stabilizes the Vata.

-The salty taste is almost uniquely derived from the salt itself, but favoring the salty taste does not mean that your food should taste like it was cured.

-Salt is already over-emphasized in the typical Western diet, so simply being mindful of tasty flavors and ensuring that your food has some salt in it is likely to be sufficient.

-Ayurveda recommends Epsom salt or high-quality sea salt over common table salt.

-Salt stimulates appetite and digestion, helps maintain moisture, promotes proper elimination, and improves the flavor of many foods.

Precaution:

The salt taste should be minimized in cases of water retention, ulcers, hypertension, aggravated blood, or excess Pitta—unbalances that may not be associated with Vata but may still be present in people with Vata constitutions or imbalances.

Reduce:

Pungent

-Pungent is a hot, spicy flavor found in chillies. Radishes, turnips, raw onions, and many, particularly are heating spices.

-It is mainly composed of fire and air elements that make it hot, dry, light, and sharp.

-It's extremely drying.

-It is exceptionally stimulating and can cause tremors, insomnia, and pain in the muscles.

-Reproductive tissues may be depleted.

-Vata imbalances such as mental confusion, dizziness, fainting, excess thirst, malaise, fatigue, emaciation, and constipation may be exacerbated.

-It can amplify Vata's high level of excitement, clarity, and expansiveness, which can lead to exhaustion, burnout, idleness, or dizziness.

-It's upward moving and lightning energy tends to destabilize the Vata.

-However, in moderation, the majority of mild spices are quite Vata-pacifying. Be warned, though, as too much of it can be drying and actually disturb Vata.

-The pungent taste is hot, dry, and light; too much of it is extremely dry to the body, exacerbates the rough consistency, and can therefore annoy Vata.

Bitter

-This is the taste that comes in the form of bitter greens (such as kale, dandelion greens, collard greens, etc.) or foods such as bitter melon, Jerusalem artichokes, burdock root, eggplant, and chocolate.

-It is mainly composed of elements of air and ether (the same elements that predominate in Vata) and is very cold, light, and dry.

-It amplifies Vata's tendency towards extreme cold.

-Dries the muscles and tissues and removes fluids from the body.

-It tends to scrape and deplete.

-It may worsen Vata disorders such as dry mouth, emaciation, fatigue, constipation, bone loss, sexual impairment, and depleted Ojas.

-Confusion, dizziness, nausea, and discomfort may be triggered.

-Vata's tendency towards feelings of boredom, separation, isolation, and loneliness may be exacerbated.

-As it is cooling, rough, drying and light, the bitter taste will further aggravate this Dosha in you.

-The bitter taste is cooling, raw, rough, drying, light, and usually lowering or catabolic—all qualities that aim to aggravate Vata.

Astringent

-This flavor has a gritty, dry feeling in the mouth–picture sipping a strong black coffee. This is also why it elevates Vata.

-It is mainly composed of elements of air and earth

-It is dry, cold, and heavy (making it particularly sensitive to Vata's delicate digestion)

-It has a specific affinity to the colon—the seat of Vata—and its qualities are inherently Vata-provoking.

-This continues to scratch and deplete.

-Vata conditions such as gas, bloating, constipation, dry mouth, speech difficulties, stiffness, spasms, emaciation, insomnia, and sexual weakness may be exacerbated.

-Physical and emotional constriction can be caused, contributing to stagnation.

-Vata's tendency to feel scattered and disorganized or even fearful, anxious, and nervous may be exacerbated.

-The astringent taste is found in legumes (such as beans and lentils), fruit (including cranberries, pomegranates, pears, and dried fruit), vegetables (such as broccoli, cauliflower, artichoke, asparagus, and turnip), grains (such as rye, buckwheat, and quinoa), spices and herbs (including turmeric and marjoram), coffee and tea. (Although all these food items are alone not suitable for Vata types, with proper food combining they can be Vata-pacifying.)

-The astringent taste is essentially a dry taste—a chalky taste that dries the mouth and may cause it to contract. For example, it's the taste you get while you're eating a green raw banana.

-Legumes are classically astringent of taste—adzuki beans, black beans, black-eyed peas, chickpeas, pinto beans, soybeans, and so on.

-The astringent flavor is dry, cold, heavy, and rugged in nature, making it understandably aggravating to Vata.

SETTING UP AN AYURVEDIC KITCHEN

We are what we eat, and Ayurvedic principles of cooking and eating prove this clearly!

The kitchen, according to Ayurveda, is the hearth, the core of a home, where food is prepared and family meets for warmth and merriment. Whether your kitchen is big or small, professional or plain, Ayurveda advises that it should be red, pulsing, and full of love.

When we consider "food as medicine," each bite provides an opportunity to rediscover what it means to be in balance with our bodies, minds, and spirits. Deciding to prepare fresh food at home will make the pathway to true wellness easier and more direct since you will be taking control over what and how you eat.

Ayurvedic Cooking puts equal emphasis on food processing as it does on the dining experience. As a result, it is important to have all the required utensils and food essentials on hand before you begin cooking.

One of the primary advantages of having an Ayurvedic kitchen is that it requires no complexity or hard work. In fact, building an Ayurvedic kitchen can be an asset that, although initially expensive, can pay for itself in the long run. Let's discuss how to set up your Ayurvedic kitchen.

I've compiled a collection of the essentials for any Ayurvedic kitchen. Once you have these things, all you need to start eating a Sattvic diet is some spices, whole grains, legumes, fresh veggies, and a little love.

Here are the essentials of an Ayurvedic kitchen:

Utensils

What you cook with is important. Mud utensils are used in traditional Indian cooking—a long-standing practice in South Asian countries. It regulates the pH of the body, offers micronutrients, and improves the taste of food. While this is no longer possible, there are still good options available.

The Importance of Ayurvedic Metals

While modern glassware and nonstick cookware are replacing conventional ways and styles of cooking in Ayurvedic metal utensils. However, one of the most essential aspects, according to the basic principles of Ayurveda, is the metal of the utensils we use to cook our meals.

Ayurvedic metals such as copper, bronze, or brass can preserve the nutritious value of your food, which is why it is recommended to use cookware and utensils made of these metals.

The importance of Ayurvedic metals and Kansa or Bronze kitchenware is stated in the popular scripture 'Rasratnasamucchaya.' The ancient civilizations used bronze to make utensils, statues of gods and goddesses, and other stuff, which is why the 3000-year era is often known as the bronze age. Kansa Kitchenware production was a kind of culture or heritage that centuries of craftsmen practiced and passed on.

Making such vessels is an elegant art that was very common in ancient times. Let's have a look at the Ayurvedic metals and how they affect our well-being.

Copper (Tamba)

We've always learned that drinking water from copper vessels is good for our health, especially digestion. Let us dig at the truth behind it. Copper is both a requisite mineral for good health and a dangerous and heavy metal. When water is stored in a copper vessel for longer than eight hours, it dissolves its positive properties in the water, and you can store water in a copper vessel for as long as you like and it would always be fresh.

The following are few advantages of using copper cookware:

- Stimulates the brain to help it perform effectively.
- Reduces joint inflammation.
- Improves the wellness of your skin and gives you a youthful glow.
- Governs digestive function.
- Get rid of the toxins in your body.
- Enhances thyroid gland activity.
- Helps in weight loss.

- Aids in the quicker treatment of wounds.
- Combat hypertension and protects cardiovascular health.
- Has cancer-preventive properties.

Brass (Pital)

The great thing about using brass utensils is that they tend to conserve the natural quality of the dishes or milk that you prepare or boil in them. Here are some benefits of using brass cookware:

- It has a calming effect that can alleviate burning sensations.
- Increases hemoglobin in the body, which improves blood quality.
- Improves the skin's health.
- Because of its excellent durability, it does not corrode quickly.

Bronze or Bell Metal (Kansa)

Bronze has been used in the creation of cookware for decades since it promotes health and well-being. Since bronze is a strong conductor of heat, it keeps food hot and nutrient-rich over a longer period of time. Let us look at some advantages of Bronze or Kansa.

- Bronze can improve indoor air quality.
- It helps to sharpen your memory by boosting your brain.
- Aids in blood purification.
- It leaves you hungry and assists in the control of your meals.
- It aids in the purification of food and the treatment of acidity.

So, use traditional metals to improve your health by countering all the negatives that degrade the nutritious content of your food and result in a failure to positively affect your health.

Instead of serving toxic chemicals from nonstick or aluminum products with your freshly cooked Ayurvedic meal, use copper, brass, bronze, stainless steel, cast iron, or stoneware cooking materials. Moreover, cookware made of high-quality materials lasts longer than cookware made of lower-quality materials.

Essential Ayurvedic Utensils include:

1-2 Pots with Lids: A two or four-quart pot would do for most purposes.

Frying Pans: 1 frying or sauté pan with a lid

Pressure Cooker: Choose the size that works best for you. An eight-quart pressure cooker should be adequate for cooking for a family of four.

A Decent Chef's Knife and a Paring Knife: If you know your way around a kitchen, you appreciate the value of getting some good knives. They are the best cooking utensils for health and they will assist you in preparing Ayurvedic dishes that are appealing to both the tongue and the eye. A chef's knife and a paring knife are needed (affectionately known as a parry knife).

Knives, like all kitchenware, are an investment. You should purchase high-quality knives with wooden handles and full-bodied steel. Remember, you just need an 8-inch chef's knife and a paring knife, not a flashy block.

And you don't have to purchase a whole knife set. It just requires two decent knives (keep them sharp by storing them away from other utensils or protected by a blade cover). Visit a store where you can test the knives before purchasing. It should feel good in your hands—not too heavy nor too light.

Rice Cooker: This gadget simplifies grain cooking by helping you to easily weigh and cook. There's no need to set a timer or think about the heat. A three-cup cooker can yield 2-4 servings. Make sure that it is labeled as having a stainless-steel interior (many of them have stainless steel exteriors, but coat the interior bowl with chemical nonstick coatings). Look for one with a steamer insert, which is a useful tool for cooking vegetables and grains at the same time. Rice may also be prepared in a pressure cooker.

Electric pressure cooker, also known as an instant pot. There are pressure cookers that will sauté, warm, and pressure cook rice, beans, soups, and other foods. They have delay start timers, so you can set it up when you leave for work in the morning to start preparing in the afternoon, so it's ready for you when you get home. Two of these can be used in place of a rice cooker and a pressure cooker.

Strainer: Choose a medium-sized strainer with a fine mesh.

1-2 Mixing Bowls: They are often offered in collections of varying sizes.

12 Large Screw-Top Jars with a Wide Mouth: Toss out the plastic storage bins and replace them with these inexpensive jars to hold your staples and homemade ghee. Since several grains look alike, write what's inside and when you bought it on the lid.

Spatulas and Other Stuff: A wooden or stainless-steel spatula, a vegetable peeler, 1-2 serving spoons, and a big wooden or stainless spoon for stirring veggies are needed.

Cutting Board: Cutting board made of wood

Small Rolling Pin: Making Chapati is easy with a small rolling pin. You can also use a glass bottle in a pinch.

Ayurvedic Food Essentials

Let's get to the foods once you've had the basic tools and utensils set up!

Having several grains and legumes on hand simplifies food preparation and reduces grocery expenses.

Consuming organically produced goods from credible sources contributes to real health. Toxins are introduced into our bodies through pesticides and genetically modified foods, disrupting proper digestion and causing diseases.

White and Brown Rice: You can stock up on white or brown rice, which is a core of any Ayurvedic food list. Consider white rice if you feel like your body is overheating, particularly as summer approaches. White rice is more cooling and lighter in quality than brown rice. Keep both in your pantry and pay attention to your body to determine what it needs at any given moment. There are several options to pick from. Basmati is my favorite.

Barley is an ideal replacement for rice in breakfast porridge. It also makes wonderful flour. As a tasty complement to your meal, consider pairing this nutty grain with pesto.

Chickpeas and Beans: Beans and chickpeas are not only high in protein and fiber, but they are also simple to store.

- **Mung Beans, Split and Whole:** Mung beans are one of the most nutritive and readily digestible legumes. Split mung cooks easily and is very digestible. It's a perfect thing to have on hand for khichdi.
- **Adzuki Beans:** If soaked for 6 to 8 hours, these cook easily in a pressure cooker.
- **Brown or Green Lentils:** More substantial than red lentils, these are a tasty lunch or dinner choice.

Whole-Wheat Flour or Your Preferred Flour: It's worthwhile to look for a decent source of freshly ground organic flour. Since Prana degrades easily after grinding, buy in limited quantities and store away from light or in the refrigerator. Or better, buy a grain mill and process your own flour from wheat berries or grains of your choice.

Mineral Salt: Although our bodies use salt to absorb nutrients and maintain proper brain functioning, not all salt is produced equal. Table salt is a heavily refined food that includes compounds that prevent us from absorbing the benefits we require from salt. It also aggravates Kapha Dosha, which causes symptoms including water accumulation and heart failure. The right combination of earth-based minerals in rock or mineral salt helps our bodies to get more out of our food (Ayurveda highly recommends Epsom salt). Note that when you cook salt with other spices, it strengthens the flavor and offers digestive support. When you add salt to cooked food, it becomes too strong for your body and aggravates Pitta Dosha.

Fruits and Vegetables: Choose colorful, fresh, and in-season fruits and vegetables as per your Prakriti!

Basic Ayurvedic Spices: Spices are the gem of Ayurvedic Cooking! All Indian households have a masala or spice box to store regularly used spices in one place. They can be obtained at any Indian grocery store.

Spices not only make food taste delicious, but they also support digestive health. Variety is the spice of life, and spices are no different to making your food taste delicious and help with gut (even overall) health. Ayurveda shines here with a whole host of spices you can use to season your food and even drinks. These come down to personal preferences, but here is a basic guide:

- Rock salt
- Cinnamon
- Black pepper
- Turmeric
- Cardamom
- Nutmeg
- Coriander
- Mustard seed
- Bay leaves
- Cumin seeds
- Fennel
- Hing

- Saffron

Be sure to store away from direct sunlight for maximum Prana and taste.

Ayurvedic Cooking Oils

The golden hue of freshly prepared ghee has a magical quality about it. Ghee is the purest essence of the earth ingredient in Ayurveda, particularly when made from local, grass-fed, organic, unsalted butter.

What Exactly is Ghee?

Ghee (or clarified butter) is the product of an alchemical phase in which butter is cooked down until the liquid evaporates and the milk solids fall to the bottom of the pan. The ghee is then squeezed into a sterilized Mason jar using a strainer or cheesecloth. Ghee does not need to be refrigerated since it is pure oil and would not go sour like dairy. If you prefer to buy ghee, there are high-quality suppliers online or at the local Indian shop or health-food store.

Ghee's Benefits

According to Ayurveda, consuming ghee has many advantages, including mental clarity and proper digestion. According to the Charaka Samhita, one of Ayurveda's classical scriptures, "the intake of ghee is recommended for those whose bodily constitution is governed by Vata and Pitta, who are suffering from diseases due to the vitiation of Vata and Pitta, those desirous of good eyesight, the elderly, infants, the weak, those desirous of longevity, those desirous of power, good skin, voice tone, nourishment, progeny, tenderness of the body, luster, Ojas, memory, intelligence, power of digestion, wisdom, proper functioning of sense organs, and those afflicted with injuries due to burns." According to the text, ghee often "augments intelligence and enkindles digestive enzymes."

Ghee, in more scientific words, assists in the preservation of balanced bacteria in the gastrointestinal tract, facilitating rapid digestion and elimination. It nourishes all the body's tissues, including the nervous system, resulting in calm energy throughout the day. Many of you who have a Vata (air and space) or Pitta (fire and water) constitution would profit the most from ghee, as it nourishes the dry, light, rough quality of Vata and the hot, light, sharp quality of Pitta.

Also, if you're worried about gaining weight by consuming ghee, don't stress! It doesn't lead to weight gain as it does not have any trans-fat but is rich in good fatty acids.

How to Make Ghee at Home

Making ghee is simple and takes just 15-30 minutes, depending on the quantity. One pound of unsalted butter, ideally organic, is all that is needed. Cook the butter in a thick, one-quart saucepan, uncovered, over medium heat until it melts. Reduce the heat to medium-low to sustain a low simmer. Keep an eye on it since the ghee can easily burn.

As the butter cooks, it will foam and sputter, and whitish milk solids will collect on the bottom of the pan. Draw the ghee off the heat once the milk solids have turned a soft golden color. Allow cooling for around 30 minutes before straining through a fine sieve or layers of cheesecloth into a clean, dry glass jar with a tight-fitting top.

Ghee can be held covered on a kitchen shelf. It does not need to be refrigerated. When using ghee, always use a clean, dry spoon or knife, as adding water or food into the ghee can trigger rancidity.

Ghee Usage

Ghee is great for cooking and sautéing. Since it is a short-chained fatty acid, it has the highest smoke point and does not contain carcinogenic free radicals when heated. This makes it one of the best oils to use in the kitchen (along with coconut oil and sesame oil).

Other Ayurvedic Cooking Oils

Other healthy oils include sesame, sunflower, groundnut, and coconut. However, each has its own Kapha/Pitta/Vata balancing properties, so choose accordingly. The best and safest oils are sesame and sunflower. Because of its properties, sesame oil is classified as "Til Sona."

Recipes

Notes:

- tbsp means tablespoon. tsp means teaspoon.
- You can use plant-based ghee if you are a vegan.
- Ayurveda highly recommends using rock salt over common table salt. So, if possible, use rock salt for the recipes.

SOUPS

Winter Vegetable Soup

This hearty Winter Vegetable Soup is flavorful and easy to prepare. You can remove any bumps or knobbly bits of the squash. You can also peel the sweet potato and squash if desired. Serve with Chapatis, freshly browned corn tortillas, or ghee-toasted whole grain bread slices.

From an Ayurvedic Standpoint:

Autumn is Vata season, with the earth starting to dry out after the summer months and a cool breeze flowing in from the impending winter. This Winter Vegetable Soup contains essential ingredients for winter Vata Dosha care. Adding leafy greens, cabbage, or any kind of legume will make it more Kapha-friendly, particularly as we approach Spring, the cleansing season.

Servings: 4-6

Time to Prepare: 40 minutes

Ingredients:

- 2 tbsp ghee oil
- 1 leek (sliced)
- 1 sweet potato (cubed)
- ½ sweet onion (chopped)
- 1 red bell pepper (chopped)
- 1 sweet dumpling squash, also called winter or carnival squash (de-seeded and cubed)
- 1 clove garlic (minced)
- 2 tbsp curry powder
- 1 cup milk or soy milk or low-fat unsweetened coconut milk
- ½ tsp salt
- 4 to 5 curry leaves

- Black pepper (to taste)

Instructions:

1. Sauté the leek, garlic, onion, and bell pepper in ghee for 8–10 minutes, or until the onion is translucent.

2. Mix the sweet potato, squash, curry leaves, salt, and curry powder in a mixing bowl. Add water just to cover and bring to a boil. Cook, uncovered, for 20–25 minutes, or until the squash is tender.

3. Stir in the milk and heat to just below boiling. Then, to taste, add fresh-ground black pepper and serve.

Butternut Soup with Coconut Milk

A creamy Butternut Squash Soup with warm garlic and ginger flavor and creaminess from coconut milk. A perfect way to stay warm in the fall and winter! Serve this full-flavored soup as an appetizer or as a smooth vegetable stew over rice with cooked greens on the side.

From an Ayurvedic Standpoint:

Butternut squash, like many other squashes in the pumpkin family, is an excellent Vata-balancing food. When all the spices have been added, it is sweet, earthy, grounding, and warms the insides pleasantly. The addition of coconut milk to the recipe provides Pitta pacification while also adding creaminess to the soup.

Servings: 2-3

Time to Prepare: 30 minutes

Ingredients:

- 1 tbsp ghee or sesame oil
- 1 tbsp fresh lime juice
- ½ cup coconut milk (if possible, use fresh instead of canned)
- 12-ounce fresh butternut squash (cubed)
- ½ cup shallots (thinly sliced)
- 2 cups water
- 1 tsp salt

- ¼ tsp ground red pepper
- 1 tbsp garlic (minced)
- 1 tbsp fresh ginger (peeled and minced)
- Ground red pepper (optional)
- Cilantro leaves (optional)

Instructions:

1. Put a large thick saucepan over medium-high heat.

2. Swirl the ghee in the pan to coat it.

3. Add the shallots and sauté for 3 minutes, or until softened, stirring periodically. Sauté for 1 more minute upon adding the garlic and ginger.

4. Add 2 cups of water, coconut milk, salt, red pepper, and squash to a boil.

5. Cook, covered, for 20 minutes, or until squash is tender, stirring periodically.

6. Place the squash mixture in a blender and blend until creamy.

7. Remove the centerpiece of the blender lid to enable steam to escape; cover the blender lid. Protect the opening in the blender lid with a clean towel (to avoid splatters).

8. Blend until fully smooth. Stir in the juice. If wanted, garnish with additional pepper and cilantro leaves.

Rice Soup with Cilantro, Ginger, Garlic, and Ghee

A balanced meal for the wintertime. Discovered in Pune, India, utilizing Sattvic Indian basmati rice that balances the physiology, nourishes the body tissues, and is simple to digest.

From an Ayurvedic Standpoint:

Basmati rice is a light, soft, smooth, soothing, and nourishing food. This rice is beneficial to all three doshas, especially Vata and Pitta.

Cilantro, ginger, and garlic help to balance Kapha, Pitta, and Vata. It relieves the effects of winter congestion and cold. Garlic is aphrodisiac and grounding for late fall Vata. Cilantro is one of the few cooling and pungent spices that promote digestion and suppress inflammation, thus lowering Pitta. Cilantro is nourishing because it has a sweet "Vipak."

Servings: 4

Time to Prepare: 20 minutes

Ingredients:

- 1 cup basmati rice
- 2 pinch black pepper
- 1 clove garlic (chopped)
- ¼ cup cilantro (finely chopped)
- ½-inch fresh ginger (chopped)
- 1 tbsp ghee
- ¼ tsp salt

Instructions:

1. Grind the rice grains in a coffee grinder to produce cream of rice.

2. In a medium saucepan, fry minced ginger and garlic in ghee.

3. Add 2 cups of water to a boil.

4. Stir in the remaining ingredients and bring to a boil.

5. Reduce the heat to low and continue to cook for 10 minutes, or until the rice is soft. Enjoy!

Spiced Vegetable Soup

This delicious winter soup is flavorful and easy to prepare. If desired, peel the sweet potato and squash. It is also beneficial to Vata, Pitta, and Kapha constitutions, as well as all dosha combinations.

From an Ayurvedic Standpoint:

This simple vegetable soup balances your Vata and is mildly cleansing as well as healing, providing natural vitamins, minerals, and proteins to nourish your body.

The flavors of curry powder and ginger give this nutrition-packed soup an authentic Indian flavor. It's an excellent source of beta-carotene, calcium, magnesium, and iron.

Servings: 3-4

Time to Prepare: 30 minutes

Ingredients:

- 2 carrots (scrubbed and chopped)
- 2 celery stalks with leaves (chopped)
- 2-3 cups fresh greens (spinach/kale/collards/chard)
- 2 small potatoes/yams (with skin, cubed)
- 1 small red beet (peeled and chopped)
- 1 cup cauliflower (chopped)
- 1 cup green cabbage (chopped)
- 1 cup of fresh tofu (cubed)
- ½ bunch fresh cilantro washed (chopped)
- 2 tsp ghee or sesame oil
- ½ tsp curry powder (easily available at any Indian grocery store)
- ½ tsp ginger (grated)
- Salt to taste (½ tsp)
- 1 small finely chopped onion (optional)
- 1 clove garlic (optional)

Instructions:

1. Heat the ghee in a medium-sized pot over medium heat.

2. Add onion and garlic. Cook, stirring frequently, for 4-5 minutes, until the garlic and onion turn golden. Mix in the curry powder and the ginger.

3. Toss in the vegetables, except the green; save the cilantro until the last step, and cook for 2-3 minutes.

4. Pour in 4-5 cups of boiling water, reduce to low heat, cover, and cook for 15 minutes.

5. Cook for 5 more minutes after adding the greens and tofu.

6. Season with salt to taste and top with cilantro.

Coconut Beet Soup

A creamy yet spicy combination makes this soup recipe a must-try at home. This rich, dark pink soup is creamy yet spicy with an earthy flavor. The coconut milk brings out the natural sweetness of the beets and is luring us into cooking it right now!

From an Ayurvedic Standpoint:

The recipe is great for building Rakta Dhatu because it is high in fiber and fats. To all people who don't like beets: they get sweeter the longer you cook them. Coconut also cuts the bitterness and adds a smooth, rich flavor. Pungent ginger complements and freshens the heaviness of coconut.

Servings: 2

Time to Prepare: 35 minutes

Ingredients:

- ¼ cup coconut flakes
- ½-inch fresh ginger
- 2 tbsp ghee
- 1 cup beets (chopped)
- ¼ tsp black pepper
- ¼ tsp salt
- Cilantro (optional)

Instructions:

1. In a blender, puree the chopped beets with an equivalent amount of water.

2. Add the puree and the remaining ingredients to a pot and bring to a boil.

3. Reduce the heat to low and continue to cook for 30 minutes.

4. Garnish with some finely chopped cilantro and serve.

Vegetable Soup with Carrots and Lime

Take a few sips of this soup and you'll fall in love with its incredible flavor, which is laced with a hint of lime. This comforting soup with fresh lime juice and ginger is extremely simple to make and can please even the pickiest eaters. This is ideal for a quick and easy lunch, a quick and easy breakfast, or a mid-day snack.

From an Ayurvedic Standpoint:

Ayurvedically, carrots with lime and other veggies are a perfect Vata-balancing mix. When cooked with Vata-balancing spices, they become more digestible.

Servings: 4

Time to Prepare: 45 minutes

Ingredients:

- ½ cup yellow onion (chopped)
- 4 whole carrots (chopped)
- 1 tbsp lime juice
- 1 cup zucchini (sliced)
- 2 whole potato (chopped)
- ¼ cup ghee
- ¼ tsp black pepper
- ¼ cup cilantro (finely chopped)
- 2 clove garlic (chopped)
- 1-inch fresh ginger (chopped)
- 1 tsp salt

Instructions:

1. In a big pot, fry the onions in the ghee.

2. Cook for another 30 seconds after adding the chopped garlic and ginger.

3. Add the remaining ingredients and fill with water to double the height of the vegetables.

4. Bring to a boil and cook for 40 minutes or until soft.

5. Garnish with cilantro, if wanted.

Note:

- This soup can also be served chilled.

Sweet Beet and Mint Soup

Sweet Beet and Mint Soup is warming, grounding, and sweet, with a luxurious purple sheen and a surprisingly spicy finish. The natural oils in mint give a startling boost to the beet root's heaviness.

From an Ayurvedic Standpoint:

Pureed foods are easier to digest. They are 'pre-chewed.' Babies, convalescent patients, and people with Vata constitutions have poor digestion. Inadequate chewing causes their stomachs to use acids to break down bigger chunks of food. While acids can easily penetrate a chunk of food, it takes time and effort for acids to penetrate a chunk of food. Thus, pureed beets are gentler than diced beets.

Beets are also rich in bioflavonoids. Bio-flavonoids have anti-allergic, anti-inflammatory, anti-microbial, and anti-cancer properties. Soon after consuming bio-flavonoids, the body attempts to eliminate them. To get rid of them, the body releases phase II enzymes, which often help get rid of mutagens and carcinogens.

Servings: 2

Time to Prepare: 50 minutes

Ingredients:

- 1 cup beets (chopped)
- 2 tbsp ghee
- ¼ cup mint
- ½ cup water
- ½-inch fresh ginger (chopped)
- ¼ tsp black pepper
- 2 pinch salt

Instructions:

1. Peel and chop the beets.

2. Bring them to a boil in a soup pot with water, ghee, and spices (except the mint).

3. Boil over low heat until thickened.

4. Puree the mixture, then stir in the fresh mint leaves.

5. Cook for another 10 minutes on low heat. Enjoy!

Kale and Carrot Soup with Ginger, Fennel, and Lime

This easy plant-based Kale and Carrot Soup has a tasty, satisfying taste. The gentle sweetness of the fennel is balanced by the spicy ginger. Coriander adds a delicate herbaceous aroma. Turmeric brings a lovely golden color to it. This nutritious vegan meal is filled with immune-boosting ingredients.

From an Ayurvedic Standpoint:

Fresh ginger is an anti-inflammatory that also increases digestion, according to Ayurvedic principles. Lime decreases stomach acidity. Soups in general are simple to digest, which is important for recovering from any digestive tract ailment. Turmeric has been shown to aid in the fight against inflammation and to improve immunity.

Servings: 4

Time to Prepare: 45 minutes

Ingredients:

- ½ lbs kale (chopped)
- 1 tbsp ghee
- ¼ tsp turmeric
- 1-inch fresh ginger (chopped)
- 4 whole carrots (chopped)
- ½ tsp fennel seeds
- 1 tsp lime juice
- ½ tsp salt

Instructions:

1. Add chopped kale and carrot in a pot and add water until vegetables are just covered.

2. Add all other ingredients and boil until kale is soft and easy to chew (Easy to chew means easy to digest).

3. Serve hot.

Potato Leek Soup with Fennel Seeds and Red Pepper Flakes

This creamy soup is smooth, rich, and seasoned. And the fiery sizzle of red pepper flakes just adds to its allure.

From an Ayurvedic Standpoint:

Cream-based soups are a decadent food that often leaves the stomach upset—but not in this case. Blended potatoes with just the right amount of ghee provide a base that is as creamy and nourishing as those of heavy cream. It is extremely beneficial for the Vata people. This lighter soup will leave you feeling calm, nourished, and rid of gas!

Servings: 6

Time to Prepare: 45 minutes

Ingredients:

- 1 cup leeks (chopped)
- 4 whole potatoes (chopped)
- 1 tbsp fennel seeds
- 2 tbsp ghee
- 1 tsp black pepper
- 2 pinch red chilli flakes
- 6 cups of water
- ½ tsp salt

Instructions:

1. In a frying pan, take 4 cups of water and the diced potatoes and leeks.

2. Bring them to a boil over medium heat.

3. After 10 minutes of boiling, strain the potatoes. Save the water.

4. Add 2 cups of water to the potatoes (to cool them before blending) and blend the potatoes and leeks together.

5. Pour the blend back into the boiling water and bring it back to a boil.

6. Add the remaining ingredients and simmer for 20 minutes on low heat.

7. Serve hot and garnish with cracked pepper and a pinch of red pepper flakes.

Buttery Carrot Soup

This traditional Buttery Carrot Soup goes well with your favorite winter salads, wraps, and even holiday entrées. Since carrots complement so many other spices, it's a versatile soup to have on hand.

You might be shocked to hear that this creamy soup is made without the use of cream. It's a light and nutritious soup and also budget-friendly.

From an Ayurvedic Standpoint:

When the body is out of balance, Ayurveda uses basic, easy-to-digest foods. Buttery Carrot Soup is easy to digest and high in fat. Onions and garlic have a calming effect on the nervous system. Black pepper gives a spicy kick.

Servings: 4

Time to Prepare: 45 minutes

Ingredients:

- ¼ cup yellow onion (chopped)
- 4 whole carrot (peeled and chopped lengthwise into ½-inch pieces)
- 2 tbsp ghee
- 1 tsp fresh thyme
- 1 bay leaf
- 2 pinch black pepper
- Water (as needed)
- 1 clove garlic (peeled)
- ¼ tsp salt

Instructions:

1. In a pot, sauté the onions with ghee.

2. Add garlic and continue to sauté for about 30-seconds, or until the garlic turns brown.

3. Place carrots in a medium saucepan, and cover with water. Bring to a boil. Reduce heat, and simmer until carrots are tender, about 20 minutes. Drain the liquid.

4. In a processor with 4 cups water, puree carrots, onions, and garlic.

4. Add this puree in the sautéed onion and garlic, along with the remaining ingredients, and bring to a boil for 15 minutes.

4. Serve hot.

Golden Turmeric Cauliflower Soup

Consider a rich, nourishing cauliflower soup that not just warms you up but also makes you feel fantastic on the inside and out. A creamy, velvety soup made of turmeric-spiced cauliflower and coconut milk. The uniqueness of this soup is not just its lively color, but also how thick and satisfying it is.

From an Ayurvedic Standpoint:

When an energy channel in our body is out of control, we can feel "dis-ease" in that region, as well as associated psychosomatic symptoms including hip pain, hormonal imbalances, stomach issues, cardiac conditions, mucus, headaches, or brain fog. This soup is a wonderful plant medicine thanks to ingredients like grounding root veggies, empowering turmeric, and heart-expanding leafy greens. Not to mention, is also Vata-pacifying.

Servings: 4

Time to Prepare: 60 minutes

Ingredients:

- 6 cups cauliflower florets
- 1 medium yellow onion (chopped)
- 3 garlic cloves (minced)
- 3 cups vegetable broth
- 2 tbsp + 1 tsp ghee or sesame oil (divided)
- A pinch of crushed red pepper flakes
- 1 tsp turmeric
- 1 tsp ground cumin
- ¼ cup full-fat coconut milk, shaken (to serve)

Instructions:

1. Preheat the oven to 450°. Toss cauliflower and garlic with 2 tbsp ghee or oil in a wide mixing bowl until well coated.

2. Toss in the turmeric, cumin, and red pepper flakes to coat uniformly.

3. Place cauliflower in a single layer on a baking sheet and bake until browned and soft, 25–30 minutes. Meanwhile, heat the remaining 1 tsp ghee in a big pot or Dutch

oven over medium heat. Cook for 2–3 minutes, or until the onion is translucent.

4. Extract the cauliflower from the oven after it has finished baking. Reserve 1 cup to top soup.

5. Put the remaining cauliflower in a medium pot with the onion and pour in the vegetable broth. Bring to a boil, then reduce to low heat and cook for 15 minutes.

6. Using an immersion blender, blend the soup to a smooth purée, or let it cool and purée in batches using a regular blender.

7. Garnish with reserved roasted cauliflower and a drizzle of coconut milk and serve.

RICE DISHES

Coconut Rice and Masala Coconut Rice

Coconut is a "Tree of Life"—a tree that is useful from head to toe and beyond. Every part of the coconut tree is used. We have learned from a range of facts and statistics that the benefit of coconut is tremendous.

Coconut Rice is a flavorful and simple rice dish made with freshly grated coconut, tempering spices, curry leaves, and rice. It is one of the most basic South Indian Foods made for festivals and special occasions.

From an Ayurvedic Standpoint:

It is said to be helpful to people with Pitta and Vata Dosha in Ayurveda. People with Kapha Dosha may still have it, but only in moderation. Coconut is a gluten-free food! Coconut flour is now accessible and can be used in a variety of recipes. It is an alkaline food with a large content of saturated fat and fiber. It also includes protein as well as minerals including calcium, iron, potassium, and magnesium. It has a low GI due to its high-fat content and can lower the overall GI of any meal when added.

Servings: 4

Time to Prepare: 30 minutes

Ingredients:

- 2.5 cup cooked rice (Sona Masoori, if possible)
- 1 fistful of peanuts
- 3 to 4 tbsp ghee
- 1½ tbsp urad dal
- 1 sprig curry leaf (10-12)
- 2 tbsp cashew nuts (crushed)
- 1 tsp mustard seeds
- 1 tbsp channa dal

- 4 to 5 green chillies
- Pinch of hing
- Few sprigs of coriander leaves
- Salt (as per taste)

Masala for Coconut Masala Rice:

- 1½ tbsp urad dal
- ½ tsp peppercorns
- 1 tsp of white til seeds
- 3 tbsp of dry copra
- ½ tsp ghee
- 4 to 5 byadgi chillies
- 1 tsp turmeric powder

Instructions:

For the Simple Coconut Rice:

1. Cook the rice first; use 2 cups of rice and around 4.5 cups of water for this. This depends on the rice; to create these rice specialties, I normally cook the rice slightly softer. However, don't make it too soft or it will ruin the flavor of any rice variety.

2. Once the rice has been cooked and the pressure has been removed, spread it out on a plate so the rice grains do not stick together.

3. Meanwhile, heat 2 tbsp ghee or coconut oil in a wok over low to medium heat, then add freshly grated coconut and fry until golden brown. Once completed, set it aside until required.

4. Then, heat the ghee in a wok and add a tsp of mustard seeds. As they splutter, add the peanuts and fry them until they change color. Eventually, add the slit green chillies and fry them until they become mildly white.

5. Now add the chana dal and urad dal. As it changes color, add a tsp of cumin and curry leaves, along with a pinch of Hing.

6. Add the salt and roasted coconut to the wok, along with the chopped coriander leaves and cooked cooled rice. Mix everything until well blended.

7. Cover the lid for 5 minutes on low heat to allow the rice to absorb all the spices.

8. Switch off the heat and serve.

To make Masala Coconut Rice:

The same ingredients as before, plus a masala powder to go along with the above-mentioned ingredients. Except for the green chillies, which should be reduced to 2 or 3.

1. In a wok, heat the ghee over low heat and add the peppercorns, urad dal, Byadgi chillies, and white til seeds for 2 to 3 minutes, or until they all change color.

2. Add the turmeric and dry copra and cook for another 2 to 3 minutes, or until the copra becomes golden brown.

3. Once finished, place it on a plate to cool.

4. Once it's cool, grind it into a powder.

5. Make the rice as said above exactly but, add this powder in step 6 with other ingredients mix well until well combined.

Masala Khichdi

Khichdi is a cornerstone of the Ayurvedic Diet. It is made up of basmati rice and mung dal and has as many varieties. Kochari is a one-pot dish that originated on the Asian subcontinent and has thousands of years of history. Spices and vegetables, when used correctly, will produce balancing results for the three bodily doshas. It has several benefits, but the fact that it is fast and simple to cook makes it a popular dish for almost every lifestyle.

Khichdi is a term used to refer to grain mixing, typically consisting of two grains. This khichdi recipe is particularly nourishing and simple to digest.

From an Ayurvedic Standpoint:

This basic meal is often used therapeutically as part of "Panchakarma," Ayurveda's ancient mind-body, cleansing, and rejuvenation ritual that helps to improve the digestive and immune systems thus maintaining equilibrium and health.

Khichdi is beneficial to all constitutions, including Vata, Pitta, and Kapha. A minor change to the seasoning is all that is needed to adapt it to your own body's needs.

Servings: 2

Time to Prepare: 35 minutes

Ingredients:

- ½ cup basmati rice
- 1 cup mung dal
- 6 cups water
- 2 tsp ghee
- 1-inch ginger root (chopped or grated)
- ½ tsp mustard seeds
- A handful of fresh cilantro leaves
- ½ tsp coriander powder
- ½ tsp turmeric powder
- ¼ tsp or so salt
- 1 pinch hing (hing)
- ½ tsp cumin powder
- ½ tsp whole cumin seeds
- 1½ cups desired vegetables (optional)

Instructions:

1. Select over the rice and dal cautiously to remove any stones. Each should be washed individually with at least two changes of water.

2. Add the 6 cups of water to the rice and dal and cook, covered, for 20 minutes, or until the rice and dal are soft.

3. Prepare any vegetables that fit your constitution while that is cooking. Cut them into bite-sized bits.

4. Cook for 10 minutes more after adding the vegetables to the cooked rice and dal mixture.

5. In a separate saucepan, sauté the seeds in ghee before they pop. Then add the remaining spices.

6. Add all the ingredients and mix thoroughly to release flavors. Mix the cooked dal, rice, and vegetable mixture with the sautéed spices.

7. Garnish with salt and fresh cilantro, if used, and serve.

Avocado Fried Rice

This recipe is extremely easy to prepare. No matter if you have leftover rice in the fridge or are making a fresh batch, this won't take long!

From an Ayurvedic Standpoint:

Avocados are beneficial to almost everyone, according to Ayurvedic principles. They're cooling and grounding for Pittas and super grounding for Vatas. It is also useful to those who suffer from dry skin and a decent source of safe oils for the body. Avocados will help you if you have a dry or sore GI tract.

Servings: 2

Time to Prepare: 15 minutes

Ingredients:

- 1 ripe avocado (chopped)
- 1 lime
- 1 cups rice (cooked)
- A handful of chopped leeks
- 3–4 tsp ghee
- 1 tsp cumin seeds
- ½ tsp brown mustard seeds
- ½ tsp turmeric
- ½ tsp chilli powder
- Additional veggies (as per choice)

Instructions:

1. Heat the oil in a pan and add the cumin and mustard seeds, cook until they start to sizzle and pop.

2. Add the leeks and cook them until they are soft. Coat the rice thoroughly with the ghee and leeks. Again, coat it properly with turmeric and chilli powder.

3. Toss the chopped avocado with the rice.

4. Make sure to mash the avocado fully into the rice. It can take some time, so don't worry about crushing the rice. That'll not happen!

5. Serve with slices of lime and enjoy!

Masala/Vegetable-Spiced Rice

Masala Rice is an Ayurvedic dish that you should try. A richly spiced rice dish with nice cashews and coconut is balanced by refreshing coriander and courgette, providing a tasty and aromatic alternative to traditional rice dishes. It's quick and easy to make, and it's the perfect recipe for when you want to try something new and healthy.

From an Ayurvedic Standpoint:

This is a basic recipe that cooks easily at the end of a long day. This recipe treats all the three doshas of Ayurveda and keeps the body in balance. Also, rice, as we already know, is a healthy, gluten-free grain.

It also includes several vitamins and minerals, such as potassium, phosphorus, folic acid, and vitamin B. It has a strong mix of dietary fiber and carbohydrates. The vegetables in it are also seasonally appropriate and have additional nutrients.

Servings: 2-3

Time to Prepare: 25 minutes

Ingredients:

- 1 cup basmati rice
- 1 cup peas
- 3 tbsp unsweetened coconut (grated)
- 2 small courgettes
- 2-3 cardamom pods
- 1 bunch of green coriander (finely chopped)
- A handful of cashews (chopped)
- 2 tbsp ghee
- 1½ tsp black mustard seeds
- 1½ tsp turmeric powder
- 1½ tsp cumin powder
- 1 pinch of cayenne pepper
- 2 bay leaves
- 2-4 cloves

Instructions:

1. Cook the rice in mildly salted water. Meanwhile, wash and clean the courgettes before cutting them into tiny cubes.

2. In a frying pan, melt the ghee. Add the remaining spices and cook over medium heat until the mustard seeds release their aroma. Add the courgettes and peas to a mixture.

2. Drain the rice and add it to the mixture if necessary. Add the cardamom pods and cloves and also the grated coconut.

3. Serve warm with chopped cashews and coriander as a garnish.

Coconut Milk Khichdi

This soothing Coconut Milk Khichdi is a vegan Ayurvedic dish that is both nutritious and tasty! I love how rich and delicious the khichdi comes out, as well as how soothing it is to consume.

This Ayurvedic khichdi recipe is suitable for lunch or dinner because it is filling without being heavy. I really like how the spices change when lightly sautéed in the pan.

From an Ayurvedic Standpoint:

In Ayurveda, Coconut Milk is commonly prescribed for both intake and application to persons with an imbalanced Vata Dosha. Coconut Milk, because of its antibacterial properties, may be used as a natural facial cleanser, particularly for people with oily or acne-prone skin.

Since an irritated Vata Dosha induces dryness in the skin and hair, integrating fresh Coconut Milk into the diet and skincare routine provides the skin with nutrient-rich nourishment that is required to replenish moisture levels and preserve natural elasticity for soft and supple skin.

Servings: 4

Time to Prepare: 65 minutes

Ingredients:

- ½ cup coconut milk (full fat)
- 1 cup split mung dal (soaked and rinsed)
- 6 cups water or low-sodium vegetable stock
- 4 cups of vegetables of your choice (like cauliflower, butternut squash, to-

matoes, and peas)
- 1 cup basmati rice
- 2 tbsp ghee or coconut oil
- 1 tbsp ginger root (freshly grated)
- 1 tbsp coriander seeds
- 1 tsp black mustard seeds
- 2 tsp cumin seeds
- 1 tsp turmeric powder
- Salt and Pepper (to taste)
- Fresh chopped cilantro for garnish (optional)

Instructions:

1. Melt ghee or coconut oil in a big pot over low heat. Add the coriander seeds, black mustard seeds, and cumin seeds and gently sauté for 5 minutes, or until the seeds tend to pop and expel their flavor.

2. Stir in the fresh ginger root and turmeric and cook for 1 minute more.

3. Toss in the remaining ingredients and stir to blend. Cover and simmer on low for 45 minutes, stirring regularly to keep the rice from sticking to the bottom and the khichari from thickening.

4. Garnish with fresh cilantro, if used, and serve warm.

Lemon Rice

Rice is a popular companion to many Ayurvedic dishes, but this variety is enriched with ingredients that are helpful during dry, Vata seasons including winter. Mustard and lemon tend to stabilize the Vata Dosha. Furthermore, the vitamin C in lemon and the natural products of turmeric all tend to improve the immune system at this period of the year.

From an Ayurvedic Standpoint:

This recipe is designed to balance all three doshas. It is simple to digest, but if eaten in abundance, it can aggravate Vata, which is why it is supplemented with lime, cumin seeds, hing, and mustard seeds. It is beneficial in cases of diarrhea, anorexia, and Irritable Bowel Syndrome. This recipe is also ideal for post-operative patients.

Servings: 2

Time to Prepare: 30 minutes

Ingredients:

- ¾ cup basmati rice
- 1½ cups water
- 1 tsp black mustard seeds
- ½ cup fresh lemon juice
- 2 tsp ghee
- ¼ tsp salt
- ¼ tsp turmeric
- A few coriander leaves (for topping)

Instructions:

1. Rinse the rice and put it in a pot of boiling water. Simmer for 20 minutes, covered.

2. Heat the mustard seeds in ghee in a separate pan until they begin to pop. Then switch off the heat.

3 Allow mustard seeds to cool before adding lemon juice, salt, and turmeric.

4. When the rice is cooked, add the spice mixture and blend properly.

5. Top with some fresh coriander leaves and serve hot.

Saffron Rice

Aromatic saffron and delicious basmati rice tempt you even before you take your first bite. This luxurious saffron rice, delicately cooked with exotic spices and ghee, is sure to soften every heart. Comfort food can be calming and relaxing at the end of a busy day. The versatility of steamed vegetables and saffron rice will relieve tension and set you up for a relaxing evening.

From an Ayurvedic Standpoint:

Saffron tastes sweet, astringent, and bitter when heated with a sweet Vipaka (post-digestive effect). It balances all three doshas, is simple to digest, and assists with food allergies. It is also very helpful for migraines, as well as for revitalizing the blood, circulation, and female reproductive system.

Servings: 5

Time to Prepare: 40 minutes

Ingredients:

- 1½ cups basmati rice
- 3 tbsp ghee
- 4 cups hot water
- 7 bits of cinnamon bark
- 1 medium pinch saffron
- 1 tbsp water
- 7 cloves (whole)
- 7 cardamom pods (whole)
- 4 bay leaves
- ½ tsp salt

Instructions:

1. Soak the saffron for at least 10 minutes in 1 tbsp water.

2. Wash the rice twice.

3. Heat the ghee in a pot over medium heat. Then stir in the bay leaves, cinnamon, cloves, salt, and cardamom for a minute.

4. Reduce the heat to minimum, add the rice, and sauté for 2 minutes with the spices.

5. Add the hot water and soaked saffron, and bring to a gentle boil. Boil for 5 minutes, uncovered. Reduce the heat to medium and partly cover.

6. Continue to boil gently for 5 minutes, stirring once or twice to avoid sticking.

7. Reduce the heat to low, cover, and simmer until tender, around 10 minutes.

8. That's it! Serve warm.

Creamy Rice Porridge with Cardamom, Cinnamon, and Nutmeg

This tasty rice dish is an ideal way to start the day for the whole family. It is grounding, warming, nourishing, easy to digest, and tridoshic, so it balances all doshas.

From an Ayurvedic Standpoint:

A warming breakfast made with light spices including cinnamon, cardamom, nutmeg, and root ginger can help stimulate the digestive fire. A balanced Agni/digestive fire ensures the body can better assimilate nutrients and remove waste. Toxins will continue to accumulate in the body because of an impaired Agni's failure to process and eliminate foods correctly.

Servings: 2

Time to Prepare: 20 minutes

Ingredients:

- ¼ cup basmati rice
- ⅛ tsp ground nutmeg
- 1 cup of milk (coconut/almond milk will also work)
- ¼ tsp ground cinnamon
- 2cm piece of root ginger (grated)
- ¼ tsp ground cardamom
- ½ tsp sugar or maple syrup (optional)
- Rose petals (for topping)

Instructions:

1. Soak the basmati rice overnight if desired, or just cook for 15 minutes in a pan with the milk and spices.

2. Until the rice is cooked and smooth, taste it and add sweetener appropriately.

3. Garnish with rose petals, if chosen, and serve warm.

Curd Rice

Curd Rice is plain, quick, and incredibly nourishing! There is no finer comfort meal than this.

During pooja, curd rice is also given to the gods. Temples in South India often offer this to the deities and give it as prasadam to the devotees.

Most south Indian households prepare this with freshly cooked rice and homemade curd or yogurt. It can, however, be made from store-bought yogurt.

From an Ayurvedic Standpoint:

Curd is highly absorbent (Grahi) in our systems, according to Ayurveda, and is capable of enhancing digestion and treating diarrhea. It helps balance Vata, digestion, sleep quality, and skin. Curd should be eaten as fresh as possible, according to Ayurveda.

Servings: 3

Time to Prepare: 30 minutes

Ingredients:

- ½ cup rice
- 2 cup curd (or yogurt)
- 1 carrot (grated)
- 1 tbsp ghee

- 2 tsp urad dal
- 1 tsp ginger (grated)
- ¼ tsp hing
- 1 tsp mustard seeds
- 1 green chilli (finely chopped)
- 10-12 curry leaves
- Salt to taste
- Pomegranate arils and peanuts (for topping)

Instructions:

1. Wash the rice properly and cook it for around 15 minutes in 1.5 cups of water. The rice should be slightly al dente.

2. When the rice is ready, mash it gently and put it aside to cool entirely.

3. Mix the cooled rice with the curd, grated carrots, green chilli, and salt. At this stage, you can add more curd or even milk if desired.

4. For the tempering, heat the ghee in a pan. Add hing, grated ginger, mustard seeds, urad dal, and curry leaves.

5. When the dal is golden brown, add it to the curd rice mixture.

6. Put it in the refrigerator for a couple of hours. Serve with pomegranate seeds and roasted peanuts on top.

7. Serve with pickles and papad cold or at room temperature.

Notes:

- Before mixing in the curd/yogurt, the rice should be freshly cooked and thoroughly cooled.
- You can also add some milk to the curd rice mixture to make it creamier.

Cauliflower Fried-Rice

Cauliflower Fried Rice is a nutritious recipe that has recently gained attention in the health and wellness culture. In this dish, cauliflower is used in place of standard rice. The result is a meal that is low in calories, grain-free, and paleo-friendly. Although it might seem to be an odd substitute, it works great! Cauliflower also retains many of the tasty flavors and is a perfect way to bring those extra vegetables into your diet!

From an Ayurvedic Standpoint:

Cooking cauliflower makes it easier to digest because the heat dissolves the fibrous cell walls that induce bloating in Vata and Kapha. Though each dosha has various dietary needs, this dish is tridoshic, which means it will help Vatas, Pittas, and Kaphas.

Servings: 5

Time to Prepare: 20 minutes

Ingredients:

- 1 head of cauliflower (chopped)
- 2 cups vegetables of your choice (chopped)
- ½ cup cooked edamame
- 1 tsp ghee
- 2 tbsp tamari
- 2 cloves garlic (minced)
- 2 green onions (diced)
- ¼ tsp cumin
- ¼ tsp turmeric

Instructions:

1. In a food processor, pulse the cauliflower until it resembles rice in texture. Alternatively, you can use a traditional cheese grater to grate the cauliflower.

3. Stir well to make sure there are no remaining chunks. It should be light and airy, with a rice-like texture.

4. Heat the ghee in a big pan over medium-high heat.

5. Add in the garlic and stir for 1-2 minutes.

6. Add the cauliflower rice, green onion, spices, edamame, vegetables, and tamari.

7. Cook for around 10 minutes, stirring constantly, until the cauliflower is tender.

8. Serve right away.

SABJI (COOKED VEGETABLES)

Sweet Potato Sabji

An easy, fast, and delicious way to incorporate healthy sweet potatoes into your diet. Sweet Potato Sabji is a dry vegetable dish made with hearty sweet potato, cumin, mustard seeds, and spinach. A basic side dish that is both tasty and simple to prepare. Once you try this recipe, it will become a regular at your dinner table!

From an Ayurvedic Standpoint:

One should always work to stay grounded and in control of their Vata through seasonal changes, as shift and transition will easily throw Vata out of balance. Including root vegetables in your diet is a perfect way to do this.

In this recipe, we use sweet potatoes, which are one of the best vegetables for Vata Dosha. The sweetness and earthiness would undoubtedly support you while you process and detox. What's the best part? It takes a total of 15 minutes to prepare.

Servings: 3

Time to Prepare: 15 minutes

Ingredients:

- 4 medium sweet potatoes (boiled, peeled, and cut into ½-inch cubes)
- 2 tbsp scraped coconut (plus more for garnish)
- 8-10 curry leaves
- ¼ tbsp lemon juice
- 2 tbsp ghee
- 1 tsp cumin seeds
- 2-3 green chillies (slit)
- 2- 3 tbsp roasted and crushed peanuts (plus more for garnish)
- Salt to taste
- ½ tsp chilli powder

- 2 tbsp chopped fresh coriander (plus more for garnish)

Instructions:

1. Heat the ghee in a nonstick pan. Mix in the cumin seeds. As they begin to change color, add the green chillies and curry leaves and sauté for a few seconds.

2. Stir in the sweet potatoes thoroughly. Mix in the peanuts.

3. Add the salt and toss well. Sauté for 3-4 minutes.

4. Add chilli powder.

5. Turn off the heat and pour in the lemon juice.

6. Add coriander and coconut.

7. Transfer in a serving bowl. Serve hot with Rotis (Indian Flatbreads) garnished with coriander, coconut, and peanuts.

Punjabi Panchratan Methi Gajar Aloo Matar Sabji

The dish is prepared without the use of onion or garlic. This is a dry sabji in the Punjabi style, made with a few spices and potatoes, peas, and winter red carrots. Yes, the name is long, but you'll remember it because of the taste it offers. For a winter meal, my mother uses to cook this over a wood fire in a Chulha (a small earthen or brick stove).

From an Ayurvedic Standpoint:

Methi Gajar Aloo Matar at Home goes well with dal-chawal (lentil-rice), pickle, and a bowl of curds for a soul-satisfying meal. It is extremely beneficial to Vatas, especially during the winter. The addition of other Indian spices enhances the flavors and improves the nutritious value of the dish.

Servings: 2

Time to Prepare: 30 minutes

Ingredients:

- ¼ cup carrots (diced)
- ¼ cups potatoes (diced)
- ¼ cup cauliflower florets (diced)

- ¼ cup green peas (freshly shelled)
- 1 cup fenugreek/Methi leaves (finely chopped)
- 1 tbsp ghee
- ¼ tsp cumin seeds
- ¼ tsp fenugreek seeds
- A pinch of hing
- A pinch of unripe mango powder (Amchoor/Khatai powder)
- ¼ tsp turmeric powder
- 1 whole green chilli
- Salt to taste

Instructions:

1. Heat the ghee in a kadhai or wok over medium heat.

2. Add in cumin, fenugreek seeds, green chilli, hing, turmeric, and potatoes until they turn soft brown on all sides.

3. Next, add all the other vegetables and cook on a very low heat, covered or open.

4. Stir regularly until all vegetables are tender and start to brown slightly if you prefer them crispy (making them crispy means overcooking).

Maharashtrian Style Takatla Palak Sabji

For lunch or dinner, serve this rich and tasty gravy sabji with steamed spinach and a hot bowl of steamed rice and ghee. It's a traditional Maharashtrian dish in which spinach (Palak) is cooked in a buttermilk gravy.

From an Ayurvedic Standpoint:

Spinach (especially raw spinach) can soften stools, overstimulate the liver, and trigger low-grade kidney pain when Vata and Pitta are out of control.

Servings: 4

Time to Prepare: 50 minutes

Ingredients:

- 2 tbsp Bengal gram (soaked in warm water for 30 minutes)
- 3 tbsp roasted peanuts (soaked in warm water for 30 minutes)

- 200 grams palak/spinach leaves (finely chopped)
- ½ cup curd or yogurt (mixed with ½ cup water to make Chaas)
- 3 green chillies (chopped)
- 2 tbsp gram flour
- 1 tbsp ghee
- ½ tsp turmeric powder
- ½ tsp hing
- ½ tsp sugar
- 3 cloves garlic (sliced)
- 1 tsp mustard seeds
- 1 tsp cumin seeds
- Salt to taste

Instructions:

1. To begin making Takatla Palak, pressure cook the chana dal and groundnuts with ½ cup water until the dal is cooked—around 3 to 4 whistles.

2. Add the chopped spinach leaves to the same pressure cooker and steam for one whistle before turning off the heat. Release the pressure instantly to keep the spinach green.

3. Heat the ghee in a pan over medium heat. Add the mustard seeds and as they begin to sputter, add the cumin seeds.

4. Add in the garlic, hing, turmeric, and chillies. Stir in the cooked spinach, dal, and peanuts with care.

5. Add Chaas (curd + water mixture), besan, salt, and sugar. Adjust the water-besan ratio to achieve the desired consistency.

6. Add the buttermilk and besan mixture to the spinach dal mixture and bring to a boil, stirring constantly, until the Takatla Palak gravy thickens somewhat.

7. When done, taste and adjust the salt and seasonings to your liking.

8. Remove from heat and place in a serving bowl.

9. Serve the Takatla Palak with hot steamed rice and some salad.

Gajar Ki Sabji (Carrot Sabji)

Gajar Ki Sabji is a basic and minimalistic Indian main course dish that is made by stir-frying and tempering fresh diced carrot pieces with Indian spices.

While most carrot recipes include carrots with other vegetables such as peas and fenugreek leaves, this basic carrot stir fry recipe stands out for its versatility and allows you to fully appreciate the natural flavor of carrots.

From an Ayurvedic Standpoint:

If one were to choose a vegetable that could be defined as a nutrient goldmine, the choice would most likely be Gajar/carrot. Carrots have a wide range of flavors, including sweet, bitter, pungent, hot, light, and sharp. Cooked carrots are sweet and warming, with a pungent Vipaka flavor, making this recipe particularly balancing for Vata and Kapha.

It is also beneficial for hemorrhoids, water absorption, and blood formation. It is an outstanding brain tonic that promotes deep thinking.

Servings: 4

Time to Prepare: 25 minutes

Ingredients:

- 4 cups carrots (finely grated)
- 2 tbsp unsweetened coconut (shredded)
- 1 small handful of fresh cilantro (chopped)
- ½ small green chilli (chopped)
- 2 cloves garlic (chopped)
- 1½-inch fresh ginger (finely chopped)
- 1 tbsp ghee
- ½ tsp black mustard seeds
- ½ tsp cumin seeds
- ½ cup water
- 1 pinch hing
- ¼ tsp salt

Instructions:

1. In a blender, add the cilantro, chilli, ginger, garlic, grated coconut, and water and blend on high until creamy.

2. Heat the ghee in a pot with mustard seeds, cumin seeds, and hing.

3. As the seeds pop, add the blended mixture and salt; let it brown slightly.

4. Stir in the carrots, cover, and cook for 10 minutes on medium heat, or until just tender. Stir it up now and then.

5. That's it! Serve warm with roti or rice.

Aloo Methi Bhaji

Aloo Methi is a quick and tasty sabji that is suitable for daily meals. It is basic but delicious and is a wholesome vegetarian dish. The gently roasted soft potatoes and the distinct bitterness of Methi leaves combine to make this Aloo Methi Bhaji a truly delightful meal.

From an Ayurvedic Standpoint:

Methi is abundant in Indian bazaars during the winter months, and it is also widely available in most Western countries. Methi or Fenugreek is a "Vatahara"–it is effective in treating Vata Dosha imbalance conditions such as neuralgia, paralysis, constipation, bloating, and many more.

Servings: 3

Time to Prepare: 50 minutes

Ingredients:

- 3 cups methi/fenugreek leaves (tightly packed)
- 500 grams (2.5 cups) potatoes (peeled and cut into 1-inch cubes)
- 1 cup onions (finely chopped)
- 1 tsp ginger (minced)
- 2 tsp garlic (minced)
- ½ tsp cumin seeds
- 2 dried red chillies (broken into halves)
- Dash of lemon juice or 1 tsp of amchur powder
- ½ tsp turmeric powder
- ½ tsp red chilli powder/cayenne pepper
- 1 tsp coriander powder
- 2 tbsp ghee

- ½ tsp salt (more as per taste)
- Pinch of hing

Instructions:

1. Heat the ghee in a heavy-bottomed Kadai/pan over medium heat; once heated, add the cumin seeds and allow them to crackle.

2. Add in the hing and dried red chillies. Sauté for a minute.

3. Add the minced ginger and garlic and sauté until fragrant.

4. Add the chopped onions and sauté until they are translucent.

5. Add the cubed potatoes, turmeric, and salt to taste. Cook, covered, over medium-low heat for 8-10 minutes, or until the potatoes are around 80% cooked, stirring occasionally in between.

6. Add in the methi leaves and mix thoroughly.

7. Stir in the ground coriander and red chilli flakes. Cook for about 5 minutes, covered.

8. Add a squeeze of lemon juice to finish the dish.

9. Mix all the ingredients well and serve hot with Chapati or as a side dish with rice, a curry of your choice, and some salad.

Notes:

- Sprinkle salt over the cleaned methi leaves and set aside for 10-15 minutes to reduce the bitterness. Squeeze out the water and add it to the recipe.
- Kasuri Methi is a decent substitute for fresh methi leaves if you can't find them. It is essentially a dry version of the fresh leaves. So, in the 6th step, replace the fresh methi leaves with ¼ cup of loosely packed dried Kasuri Methi, dry roasted on low heat and crushed between your palms.

Ayurvedic Green Bean Sabji

Ayurvedic Green Bean Sabji is a tasty recipe that is high in protein, vitamins, and minerals. Green beans, shredded coconut, and ghee are the main ingredients in this dish, along with a few others. It is easy to prepare at home at any time.

From an Ayurvedic Standpoint:

Green beans are sweet, sweet, and astringent. If consumed in abundance, they may upset the Vata Dosha. They have a proclivity to trigger gas and constipation. But since this recipe is made with hing and cumin seeds, it does not affect the Vata Dosha. However, Vata person should eat it in limit.

Servings: 5

Time to Prepare: 20 minutes

Ingredients:

- Half an onion (chopped)
- 2 cloves garlic (finely chopped)
- 4 cups of green beans (cut off the ends of the beans and slice on the diagonal into very small pieces)
- 1 tbsp coconut (shredded)
- 2 tbsp coriander (chopped)
- ½ tsp cumin seeds
- ½ tsp black mustard seeds
- 1-inch piece of fresh ginger (finely chopped)
- 2 tbsp ghee
- ½ tsp masala powder
- ¼ tsp turmeric
- A pinch of hing
- ½ tsp salt

Instructions:

1. Add the garlic, ginger, coconut, and coriander to a blender and blend thoroughly. Let it aside.

2. In a medium saucepan, heat the ghee and add the cumin seeds, mustard seeds, and hing.

3. As the seeds begin to pop, add in the turmeric, masala powder, and chopped onions. Stir constantly until the onion softens and becomes pink.

4. Now add the blended paste, salt, and green beans.

5. Cover and cook on low heat until softened. This will take about 2 minutes, and your

Ayurvedic Green Bean Sabji is ready to be served.

Gobi Matar

In our Indian household, Gobi/cauliflower is a common sabji. This is something we make at least once a week. It's a basic Indian stir-fry with winter green peas.

Serve it with plain roti and dal for a filling dinner.

From an Ayurvedic Standpoint:

Cauliflower and potatoes may be gas-producing for Vata individuals; but, with the addition of ghee and spices, this dish becomes digestible for Vata individuals when consumed in moderation. They enrich it by making it more nourishing and grounding for Vata. This recipe is also perfect for Pitta people, but it is not recommended for Kapha people.

Servings: 4

Time to Prepare: 45 minutes

Ingredients:

- 500 gm cauliflower (floret)
- 2 whole potato (peeled and cut into tiny pieces)
- 1 cup green peas
- 2 tbsp onion (finely chopped)
- 1 tsp ginger (finely chopped)
- 1 tsp Methi/fenugreek leaves
- 2 tbsp ghee
- 2 tsp red chilli powder
- 1 tbsp coriander powder
- 1 tbsp turmeric powder
- Salt to taste
- 1 sprig of coriander leaves (for garnishing)

Instructions:

1. Add the florets to a large bowl and cover with hot water.

2. Stir in a tsp of salt. Set aside for 10 minutes.

3. In a bowl, add the diced potatoes and soak them in cold water.

4. Heat the ghee in a kadhai or nonstick pan. Add the fenugreek seeds and as they begin to sputter, add the ginger and onion.

5. Now stir in the cauliflower florets, peas, and potatoes and fry for a few minutes.

6. Cook for 2-3 minutes, covered.

7. Stir in the turmeric, red chilli powder, coriander powder, and salt, and thoroughly mix all the spices and veggies. Adjust the salt to taste.

8. Cover with a tight-fitting lid and cook for 5 to 6 minutes on low heat. Turn off the heat.

9. Garnish with coriander and serve hot with Chapati or Poori.

Palak Paneer

Palak Paneer is a traditional Indian dish that is gaining popularity around the world. This saucy and flavorful dish made with spinach and cottage cheese (paneer) is well worth learning how to make.

From an Ayurvedic Standpoint:

Paneer is beneficial to the Vata and Pitta Dosha, while spinach is great to the Kapha Dosha. What are the advantages of Palak Paneer in terms of health? It is high in iron, vitamins A, K, C, and E, magnesium, folate, calcium, and protein. So, in addition to pampering your taste buds, it also benefits your well-being!

Servings: 3

Time to Prepare: 40 minutes

Ingredients:

- 150 gm paneer (chopped into cubes)
- 2 cups spinach (chopped)
- ½ cup onions (finely chopped)
- ½ cup tomatoes (chopped)
- 4 tbsp ghee
- 1 tsp ginger
- 2-3 cloves garlic

- ½ tsp dried fenugreek leaves
- 2 pieces of green cardamom
- 1 tsp cumin seeds
- 2 cloves
- 1 tsp cinnamon powder
- 1 tsp coriander powder
- A pinch of salt

Instructions:

1. To begin, mix the spinach and tomatoes in a blender to make a smooth paste.

2. Next, heat 2 tbsp ghee in a medium pan.

3. Add cinnamon, cardamom, cumin seeds, and cloves in it.

4. Once the cumin seeds pops, introduce the ginger and garlic.

5. Add in the onions.

6. Add the coriander powder and fenugreek once they've finished cooking.

7. Add a cup of water to allow the mixture to thicken. Then pour the spinach paste.

8. Once the spinach is cooked, add the paneer.

9 Allow it to simmer for 5 minutes.

10 Serve with rice or Chapatis.

Sev Tamatar Ki Sabji

Rajasthani Sev Tamatar Sabji is a tasty side dish that comes in handy when you don't have any veggies on hand but also want to make a nutritious dinner. This sabji is made with juicy tomatoes sautéed with desi masalas and eaten with a heaping pile of thick besan sev.

It goes well with any Indian bread, but particularly roti and parathas. However, service it immediately since the sev can get soggy with time.

From an Ayurvedic Standpoint:

While Ayurveda claims that tomatoes increase all three doshas (Vata, Pitta, and Kapha), especially Pitta, the unfavorable impact of tomatoes can be reduced by cooking them with spices such as turmeric, chilli, and cumin seeds. Sev made from besan stimulates Kapha, energizes, is easy to digest, and reduces Pitta and Vata.

Servings: 4

Time to Prepare: 30 minutes

Ingredients:

- 1 cup besan sev (thick variety, can be found in any Indian grocery)
- ½ cup onion (chopped)
- 1 cup tomato (chopped)
- 1 tsp ginger (grated)
- 1 tsp garlic (chopped)
- 1 tbsp lemon juice
- 3 tbsp ghee
- 1 tsp cumin seeds
- 2 tbsp fresh coriander (chopped)
- ½ tsp hing
- 2-3 green chilli (slit into half)
- 2 tsp coriander powder
- ½ tsp turmeric powder
- 1 tsp Kashmiri red chilli powder
- Salt to taste

Instructions:

1. Heat the ghee in a pan.

2. When the ghee is hot enough, add the cumin seeds and hing and cook for a few seconds, stirring constantly.

3. Fry for a minute after adding the green chilli, ginger, and garlic.

4. Add the onion and fry until it becomes translucent.

5. Add the tomato and cook until it is mushy.

6. Season with salt, coriander powder, turmeric powder, Kashmiri red chilli powder.

7. Pour in ½ cup of water and cook until the ghee breaks from the side.

8. Now add 1 cup of water to the sabji and bring to a boil.

9. Remove from the heat and stir in the sev and lemon juice.

10. Garnish with fresh coriander, if desired.

11. Serve right away.

Notes:

- Always make this sabji fresh, as it tastes the best when served hot.
- Always use sev at the end and just give it a mix. Because if you cook the sev, it will become soft in the curry itself and will taste bad.

Kaju Mutter Masala

The cashews make it the fantastic treat that it is. The Kaju Mutter Masala is a cashew lover's dream, with crispy cashews and soft green peas in a rich, tangy masaledar gravy.

The gravy is very rich, with cashews, tomatoes, fresh cream, and spice powders as the key ingredients.

From an Ayurvedic Standpoint:

Cashews are sweet and heavy, and they can relax your nerves as well as satisfy your appetite. The crescent-shaped cashew is dense and warm, boosting strength and keeping you feeling nourished, particularly during the cooler months. With each bite, these crunchy nuts become creamy and smooth.

These nuts are native to Brazil and are technically the seeds of the cashew apple. Since cashews are related to poison ivy, certain people are very allergic to them. They balance Vata and Pitta but are too heavy and difficult to digest for Kaphas.

Servings: 4

Time to Prepare: 35 minutes

Ingredients:

- 2 cups tomatoes (roughly chopped)
- 1 cup Kaju/cashew nuts
- 2 tbsp ghee
- 1 tbsp fresh cream
- 1¼ cups green peas (boiled)

- 1 tsp dried fenugreek leaves (kasuri methi)
- 1 bay leaf
- 1 tsp garlic paste
- ½ tsp ginger paste
- ½ tsp chilli powder
- ½ tsp garam masala
- Salt to taste

Instructions:

1. Heat the ghee in a nonstick pan over low heat, then add the cashews and sauté for 3 minutes. Extract and set aside to cool.

2. In a deep nonstick pan, add the tomatoes and ½ cup of water, blend, and cook for 6 minutes, stirring periodically, over medium heat. Set this mixture aside to cool.

3. In a blender, add this mixture and the cashew nuts and blend until smooth. Keep aside.

4. Heat the ghee in the same pan over medium heat, then add the bay leaf, garlic paste, and ginger paste and sauté for 30 seconds.

5. Stir in the tomato-cashew nut mixture and cook for 2 minutes on medium heat, stirring periodically.

6. Stir in the chilli powder, garam masala, dried fenugreek leaves, and salt, and cook for 1 minute on medium heat.

7. Stir in the fresh cream, green peas, and ¼ cups of water, then cook for 2 minutes on medium heat, stirring periodically.

8. Stir in the crispy cashews and cook for 2 more minutes on medium heat, stirring periodically. Serve warm.

CURRIES

Mung Dal Curry

Dals come in a range of varieties in Indian cuisine. And, since they are grown all over the world, there may be a hundred different dal recipe variations. This Mung Dal Curry is a simple yet tasty dish along with fried rice (it's my favorite curry).

From an Ayurvedic Standpoint:

Dals are hearty soups that are ideal for Vata all year. Yellow mung is pleasant and cooling, and it primarily calms the Vata and Pitta Dosha. It encourages strength and is very easy to digest. The seasonings in this soup help to balance the soup's drying, light, and astringent qualities, which could aggravate Vata.

Servings: 5

Time to Prepare: 20 minutes

Ingredients:

- ¼ cup non-fried peanuts (unsalted)
- 2 cups mung dal (make sure that there's no stone in the dal)
- 4 tbsp ghee
- 1-inch ginger (finely chopped)
- 1 tsp whole cumin seeds
- 2 sliced green chillies
- ½ tsp turmeric powder
- ½ tsp hing powder
- 1 tsp salt
- ¼ tsp sugar

Instructions:

1. Wash the dal thoroughly with running water and then keep it aside.

2. In a deep pan, heat the ghee and fry the cumin, green chillies, and hing until the seeds crack.

3. Add the remaining ingredients and dal to this pan, fill with water, and cook until the dal is fully cooked. Feel free to add boiling water to achieve the desired consistency for the dal.

4. Serve with roti or rice.

Notes:

- Remember that for dal to be adequately cooked, it must be slightly overcooked—the seeds should all be one and not individually discernible, however, it should not all be a "paste."

Ayurvedic Thai Green Vegetable Curry

Curries can seem daunting, but they are very simple to prepare. This Ayurvedic Thai Green Vegetable Curry has a gentle taste with a lot of depth and mild flavoring. It has a great flavor, balances all three doshas, and is simple to make.

From an Ayurvedic Standpoint:

This dish can be prepared in a tridoshic way. The coconut milk used is both nourishing and soothing for the Vata and Pitta Dosha. The spices used are digestive and aid in the curry's digestion. Ginger, garlic, green chillies, pepper, and lemongrass are a few examples of these spices and herbs. Coriander seeds and cilantro are both digestive and cooling, balancing out some of the pungent and heating spices described earlier.

Servings: 4

Time to Prepare: 35 minutes

Ingredients:

- 4 cups of diced vegetables of your choice (like carrots, cauliflower, baby corn, zucchini, celery, onions)
- ½ cup coconut milk
- 1 tbsp sugar
- 1 cup tofu
- 1 tbsp ghee

- 1 handful basil leaves
- 1 tbsp soy sauce
- 1 tsp black peppercorns
- 3 tsp lemongrass stalks
- 1 tbsp ginger
- 3 tbsp spring onions
- 2 handfuls of coriander leaves
- 5 garlic cloves
- 4 green chillies (or more as per taste)
- 1 cup spinach leaves(chopped)
- 1 tsp coriander seeds
- 1 tsp cumin seeds
- 1 tsp lime zest
- 1 tbsp lime juice
- Salt (to taste)
- 1 tbsp rice flour (optional)

Instructions:

1. Grind these ingredients—coriander, cumin, black pepper, lemongrass, ginger, garlic, green chillies, spring onions, coriander, lime zest, lime juice, basil leaves, and soy sauce—in a grinder with a little water. Pour this into a clean, dry glass container and refrigerate. (While held refrigerated, this may be used for up to 2 weeks.)

2. Warm the ghee in a wide pan over medium heat. Sauté the tofu and onions until the onions are translucent.

3. Add the vegetables, beginning with the ones that take the longest to cook. Add in the salt and sugar. Increase the heat to medium-high and continue to stir constantly.

4. Cook for 2-3 minutes after adding 3 tbsp green curry paste.

5. Add coconut milk (store-bought or homemade) and spinach, and bring to a boil. If the consistency is too fluid, make a paste of rice flour and water, add it to the gravy, and bring it to a boil.

6. Serve immediately with brown or white rice.

Curried Chickpea with Carrots

Curries that are heavy and hearty are a specialty in Indian home cooking. Chickpea

Curry, in particular, provides a nourishing warmth. The explanation for this is because chickpeas have more tryptophan than other legumes. Tryptophan is a necessary amino acid that aids in regulating sleep and emotions. Using chickpeas brings a calming, comfort food feeling to this meal, making it satisfying.

From an Ayurvedic Standpoint:

Any flavor you might think of has a place in Indian curry, whether it's salty, spicy, sweet, sour, or flavorful. Mild chickpeas and sweet carrots can be spiced up with pungent ginger, cayenne pepper, cinnamon, cumin, bitter fenugreek, herbal cloves, cardamom, and earthy onions to benefit Vata Prakriti!

Servings: 3

Time to Prepare: 30 minutes

Ingredients:

- 2 whole tomatoes (crushed, keeping the liquid)
- ⅓ cup yellow onion (finely sliced)
- 1 tbsp ghee
- 6 whole carrots (crushed)
- 1 cup chickpea (rushed)
- ½ tsp black salt
- ¼ tsp cayenne powder
- ¼ tsp cinnamon
- ½ tsp cloves
- ½ tsp cumin
- ¼ tsp fenugreek
- ½ tsp ginger

Instructions:

1. Grind all the spices and mix with a small amount of water to make a paste.

3. Heat ghee in a pan and sauté finely sliced onion. When the onion starts to brown, add the spices and stir.

4. Sauté for 15 seconds before adding crushed tomato, chickpeas, carrots, and water.

5. Get the water to a boil. Reduce the heat to low and continue to cook until the carrots are tender.

6. Serve warm.

Indian Coconut Curry

Here's a tasty Ayurvedic Cooking recipe with some healthy earth components that can be really grounding and balancing. This one can be very warming, particularly on a cold winter day.

From an Ayurvedic Standpoint:

This Indian Coconut Curry recipe can rejuvenate and regenerate the body's tissues. It is suitable for all doshas or constitution types, but due to the earth elements in this recipe, it is particularly beneficial for Vata Dosha.

Servings: 3

Time to Prepare: 25 minutes

Ingredients:

- 2 tbsp coconut (finely shredded)
- 1 cup fresh coconut milk
- 1 yam (medium, chopped in small cubes)
- 1 potato (medium, chopped in small cubes)
- 1 tsp ginger (grated)
- ½ tsp coriander seeds
- ¼ tsp cumin powder
- 2 tbsp ghee
- A pinch of salt
- 2 pinches of fennel seed powder
- A pinch of freshly ground black pepper
- 2 pinches of cardamom powder
- A pinch of cinnamon
- ¼ cup of raw or slightly roasted cashews (optional)
- Cilantro (optional)

Instructions:

1. In a medium pan, heat the ghee and sauté the coriander seeds, cumin, cinnamon, cardamom, fennel, and salt.

2. After the aromas have been emitted, add the ginger and sauté for 1 to 2 minutes.

3. Now add the sweet potato and yam and sauté for 1 to 2 minutes.

4. Add the coconut milk and continue to cook until the potatoes are tender.

5. Turn off the heat and stir in the coconut and cashews.

6. End with a dash of black pepper.

7. Garnish with cilantro, if desired.

Creamy Coconut Lentil Curry

This simple Creamy Coconut Lentil Curry is a nutritious vegan recipe that is ideal for a dinner. It takes less than an hour to make (mostly hands-off time) and is filled with delicious Indian flavors.

From an Ayurvedic Standpoint:

Lentils are delicious, astringent, cooling, and balancing for all doshas, especially when cooked with warming spices like ginger, cumin, and coriander.

Lentils are also called a Sattvic nutrient, which means they are both soothing and nourishing to the mind and body. Enjoy this basic and delicious meal as a treat for yourself. And, as we all know, coconut is extremely beneficial to Vata.

Servings: 6

Time to Prepare: 55 minutes

Ingredients:

- 1 cup brown lentils (dried)
- A few handfuls of cherry tomatoes
- 1 head of garlic (10–12 cloves, chopped)
- 28-ounce of tomatoes (crushed)
- 2 tbsp ginger (chopped)
- 1 cup cilantro (chopped)
- 1 tbsp ghee (or coconut oil)
- 1 tbsp cumin seeds
- 1 tbsp coriander seeds
- 1 tbsp turmeric

- 2 tsp sea salt
- 3 cups of water
- 15-ounce coconut milk
- 1–2 tsp cayenne powder (optional)

Instructions:

1. In a big pot or pan, heat the ghee or coconut oil over medium-high heat.

2. Toast the cumin and coriander seeds for 45 seconds, or until they begin to brown.

3. Next, brown the garlic in the pot for around 2 minutes.

4. Add the crushed tomatoes, ginger, turmeric, and sea salt to the pot and cook for 5 minutes, stirring occasionally. Bring the lentils and, if using, the cayenne powder, as well as the water, to a boil in a pot.

5. Reduce the heat to minimum, cover the pot, and cook for 35-40 minutes, or until the lentils are tender.

6. Stir the lentils a couple of times to keep them from sticking to the bottom of the container. If the curry seems to be drying out, add an additional ½–1 cup of water.

7. Once the lentils are soft and the curry is moist, add the coconut milk and cherry tomatoes and switch to medium heat.

8. Remove from the heat, stir in the cilantro, and serve warm.

Dum Aloo (Potato and Pea Curry)

Dum Aloo is a tasty Indian curry of potato and green peas that goes well with phulka roti, chapati, or paratha for lunch or dinner. It is a potato and pea curry, which is probably India's most common vegetable curry.

From an Ayurvedic Standpoint:

When peas are used in the regular diet, they tend to increase appetite. Loss of appetite is caused by Agnimandya in Ayurveda (weak digestion). It is induced by an imbalance of the doshas Vata, Pitta, and Kapha, which results in inadequate digestion of food. This triggers inadequate gastric juice secretion in the stomach, resulting in appetite loss. Peas' Deepan (appetizer) property stimulates digestion and improves appetite. Potatoes, which may be too heavy for Vatas, are lightened up with spices like turmeric and cumin. It is supported further by the addition of salt and fenugreek.

Servings: 4

Time to Prepare: 35 minutes

Ingredients:

- 1 cup peas
- 1 cup water
- 5 cups potatoes (peeled and cut into small cubes)
- ¼ cup ghee
- 1½ tsp cumin seeds
- 1 tsp turmeric
- 1 tbsp fresh ginger (minced)
- ¼ tsp ground fenugreek
- Salt to taste
- Chopped cilantro (optional)
- Pinch of hing (optional)

Instructions:

1. Heat the ghee in a pan.

2. Add the hing, ginger, and cumin seeds and sauté for 1 minute, stirring constantly, over low heat.

3. Sauté for 5 minutes, stirring continuously, after adding the potatoes.

4. Mix in the water, turmeric, fenugreek, peas, and salt to taste.

5. Cover and cook for 15-20 minutes, or until the vegetables are tender.

6. Adjust the salt as per your taste.

7. Garnish with cilantro and serve with rice or Indian flatbread (roti).

Tridoshic Vegetable Curry

This simplistic curry will please your taste buds and is a summer-time must! Served with a rainbow of vegetables, you'll appreciate the anti-aging, anti-cancerous, and anti-inflammatory properties of this delightful curry. Furthermore, this delectable vegetable curry balances all three doshas, making it an excellent option for any season!

From an Ayurvedic Standpoint:

The other vegetables and curry spices round out the cooling properties of the peas and potatoes. This tiny volume of yogurt, thinned with water, is generally well absorbed by all doshas and helps digestion. Try to use tender peas rather than frozen peas wherever possible since they are more balancing for Kapha and Vata.

Servings: 4

Time to Prepare: 25 minutes

Ingredients:

- 2 cups of green string beans or asparagus (cut into 1-inch pieces)
- ½ cup yogurt
- 1 cup of fresh peas
- 1 cup carrot (diced)
- 1 cup potatoes (diced)
- 1.5 cups of water
- 2 tsp ghee
- 2 tsp cumin seeds
- 2 tsp black mustard seeds
- 2 tsp turmeric
- 1 tsp coriander powder
- 1 tsp sea salt

Instructions:

1. Heat the ghee in a large pan. Add the mustard and cumin seeds. As the mustard seeds pop, add the turmeric.

2. Next, add all the vegetables and the water. (If using frozen peas, wait until the majority of the vegetables are nearly done before adding them.)

3. Cook, covered, for 15-20 minutes, or until the vegetables are tender.

4. Stir in the yogurt and the rest of the ingredients.

5. Continue cooking, uncovered, on low heat for another 15-20 minutes.

6. Serve with rice or other grains.

Spicy Spinach, Kale, and Cauliflower Curry

This recipe is incredibly flavorful, thanks to the wonderful variety of spices, and is sure to energize your appetite and get your blood pumping. It is delicious enough to eat on its own, but it also goes well with Chapatis.

This vegetable curry recipe contains a soothing combination of cauliflower, kale, and spinach, rendering it beneficial to cardiac health, liver health, colon health, weight loss, and iron deficiency.

From an Ayurvedic Standpoint:

This curry is soothing for Vata because it is warming, (slightly) oily, and well-spiced, and reducing for Kapha because it is light, spicy, and energizing. While cauliflower and kale can often aggravate Vata, the well-cooked quality of this recipe, as well as the complementary ingredients (i.e., heating spices, coconut, sesame oil, etc.), can help to add harmony, making it simple to digest, less drying, but a little more grounding.

Servings: 4

Time to Prepare: 30 minutes

Ingredients:

For the sauce:

- 1 cup water
- 1 tbsp coconut (shredded)
- 2 tsp serrano pepper (chopped)
- ½ cup well-packed cilantro (chopped)
- 2 tbsp ginger (coarsely chopped)
- 4 tbsp lime juice
- ½ tsp cumin seed
- 1 tsp Vata Churna (or plain turmeric)
- ¼ tsp salt

For the sauté:

- 4 cups cauliflower (chopped)
- 4 well-packed cups spinach (chopped)

- 2 cups kale (well-steamed and chopped)
- ½ cup onion (minced)
- 2 garlic cloves (minced)
- ¼ cup water
- ¼ cup cilantro (finely chopped)
- 2 tbsp coconut (shredded)
- 2 tbsp ghee
- ½ tsp cumin seed (whole)
- ¼ tsp salt
- ½ tsp brown mustard seed (whole)
- ⅛ tsp freshly ground black pepper

Instructions:

To make the sauce:

1. Fill a blender with 1 cup water.

2. Add the chopped serrano pepper, cilantro, and ginger to the blender.

3. Add the Vata Churna (or turmeric), cumin, salt, shredded coconut, and lime juice.

4. Blend for 1 to 3 minutes on high, or until a dense, smooth liquid is formed.

5. Set aside the curry sauce until needed for the sauté.

To make the sauté:

1. Heat the ghee in a wide, deep sauté pan over medium heat.

2. Add the cumin seed, brown mustard seed, black pepper, garlic, and onion. Sauté, stirring constantly, for 3 minutes, uncovered.

3. Stir in the cauliflower, kale, and ¼ cup water. Continue to sauté, uncovered, for 3 minutes over medium heat, stirring regularly.

4. Stir in the curry sauce and the spinach. Cover the pan and stir well. Increase the heat marginally to medium-high. Cook for 3 minutes, stirring just halfway through.

5. Uncover the pan and simmer for another 6–7 minutes, stirring every 2–3 minutes.

6. When the curry is ready to your taste, switch off the heat but leave the pan on the

hot burner. Blend in the chopped cilantro, shredded coconut, and salt. Stir well until all the ingredients are mixed.

7. Taste the dish and season with additional salt, pepper, or lime juice if needed.

8. Serve this veggie curry as a side dish to any savory meal, or as a light, nutritious breakfast, lunch, or dinner on its own. This recipe is better served during the autumn, winter, and early spring seasons.

Ayurveda Pumpkin Curry

This delicious Pumpkin Curry is ideal for all doshas. It's not only nutritious, but it's also a naturally vegan pumpkin curry recipe—no soya products, chemicals, or genetically engineered ingredients are used.

From an Ayurvedic Standpoint:

We are in a season when Vata can quickly get out of control, and pumpkins are beneficial to all three doshas (Vata, Pitta, and Kapha)

Pumpkins are high in vitamins A, C, and E, all of which are anti-oxidants. In addition to antioxidants, they have a high fiber content. Vitamin A promotes healthy skin and immune function, while fiber aids in blood glucose regulation. Pumpkins also contain minerals like magnesium and potassium, which tend to regulate blood pressure and relax muscles, thus protecting the circulatory system. They are low in fat and high in omega-3 fatty acids, which are anti-inflammatory.

Pumpkin's anti-oxidant and anti-inflammatory effects make it beneficial in a variety of health-related ways. Pumpkin compounds have been studied for cancer prevention and care. Pumpkins have also been shown to help in blood sugar control and insulin regulation. Furthermore, pumpkin's antioxidants and anti-inflammatory compounds seem to promote cardiovascular and cardiac well-being.

Servings: 3

Time to Prepare: 60 minutes

Ingredients:

- 2 cups pumpkin (peeled and cubed)
- ½ tsp garam masala

- ½ tsp each of mustard and cumin seed
- 2 tsp coconut (desiccated)
- ½ tsp fenugreek
- 1 tbsp ghee
- 1 tsp ground peanut
- 2 tsp jaggery
- ½ tsp ginger powder
- ½ tsp turmeric powder
- Salt to taste
- Fresh coriander (for garnishing)

Instructions:

1. Heat the ghee in a pan and add the mustard seed, fenugreek, cumin seed, ginger powder, and turmeric, stirring constantly until the mustard seeds pop.

2. Add pumpkin and mix for 1-2 minutes, or until well coated. After that, add enough water to cover the pumpkin.

3. Season with salt, desiccated coconut, ground peanut, and garam masala. Stir, cover, and cook for around 20 minutes on medium to low heat.

4. Add jaggery at the end and garnish with fresh coriander.

Shahi Paneer

It's a delicious North Indian curry made with paneer (cottage cheese) and a spicy tomato-based gravy laced with spices. This is a popular recipe that has been passed down across centuries and has been a mainstay of Indian cuisine since the time of the Moguls. To add rich texture and taste to this Shahi Paneer recipe, a tomato gravy based on cashew nuts is used.

It's a thick, onion-tomato paneer gravy dish that goes well with roti, naan, kulcha, paratha, or pulao. Using blanched onions and freshly ground spices is important in this fragrant curry.

From an Ayurvedic Standpoint:

The bones and joints are considered a Vata site in the body as per Ayurveda. Joint discomfort is caused by a Vata Dosha imbalance. Paneer's Vata balancing properties help to prevent joint discomfort when consumed often. Paneer is also high in protein, calcium, and phosphorus, which aid in the formation of healthy bones and, as a result, the reduction of joint pain.

Servings: 4

Time to Prepare: 40 minutes

Ingredients:

For the onion-tomato puree:

- 2 tomato (chopped)
- 1 onion (sliced)
- A handful cashews
- 1 cup water
- 1 tbsp ghee
- 3 clove garlic
- 1-inch ginger (chopped)
- 2 pods cardamom
- 1 pinch cinnamon
- 1 pod black cardamom
- 3 cloves
- 1 tsp salt

For curry:

- ¼ cup cream
- 15 cubes paneer
- 1 tbsp butter
- ½ tsp shahi jeera
- ½ tsp kasuri methi (crushed)
- 1 bay leaf
- ¼ tsp turmeric
- ¼ tsp garam masala
- 1 tsp Kashmiri red chilli powder
- few threads saffron

Instructions:

1. First, heat 1 tbsp ghee/butter in a kadhai and sauté 2 pods cardamom, 1-inch cin-

namon, 1 pod black cardamom, and 3 cloves.

2. Add in 1 onion, 3 garlic cloves, a handful of cashews, and 1-inch ginger.

3. Sauté for a few minutes, or until the onion softens.

4. Add 2 tomatoes and sauté for a few more minutes.

5. Next, add 1 cup of water and 1 tsp salt. Mix thoroughly.

6. Cover and cook for 20 minutes, or until fully softened.

7. Allow to cool completely and transfer to a blender. Without adding any water, blend to a smooth paste.

8. Sieve the puree to ensure it is clean and creamy. Set aside.

9. Heat 1 tbsp ghee/butter in a big kadhai and sauté ½ tsp shahi jeera and 1 bay leaf.

10. Keeping the flame low, add ¼ tsp turmeric and 1 tsp chilli powder.

11. Sauté the spices until fragrant, then add the prepared tomato-onion puree and blend well.

12. Stir in ¼ cup cream and mix until it is well blended.

13. Mix in 15 cubes paneer and a few threads of saffron. Cover and cook for 5 mins, or until the flavors are well absorbed.

14 Add ½ tsp kasuri methi and ¼ tsp garam masala. Mix thoroughly.

15. Finally, serve this delicious shahi paneer with roti, pulao, or naan.

Beetroot and Carrot Curry

A simple curry with appealing flavors. Allow the ginger and curry in this flavorful carrot and beet curry dish to warm you all the way through.

From an Ayurvedic Standpoint:

Root vegetables are grounding and healing for the autumn season, and they tend to soothe irritated Vata. Chukandar (Beetroot) and Gajar (Carrot) are both sweet and have warming powers. They work together to support digestion and cleanse the stomach and intestines.

This Beetroot and Carrot Curry is not only tasty, but it is also an excellent way to minimize Vata's effects on the body. It is nourishing and energizing and can be enjoyed throughout the autumn and winter season.

Servings: 4

Time to Prepare: 35 minutes

Ingredients:

- 2 medium-size carrots
- 1 large beet (partially or fully boiled)
- 1.5 cups of water (more if you want soupy)
- 1 tsp ghee
- 2-inch ginger (grated or made to a paste)
- ¼ cup peanuts (toasted and crushed)
- A pinch of hing
- 1 tsp cumin seeds
- 2 red dry chilli pepper (or some red crushed pepper)
- fresh cilantro (chopped, for garnishing)
- Salt to taste

Instructions:

1. Peel the skin of the boiled beet and dice the beet. Keep aside.

2. Heat ghee in a pan. Add in the hing, dry red chilli, and cumin seeds.

3. As the seeds sizzle and the pepper turn a darker shade, add the diced carrots and beets to the pan.

4. Add salt and grated ginger and cook on high for a couple of minutes while tossing occasionally.

5. Add water and peas (if you want) and simmer uncovered or partially covered until carrots are tender.

6. Adjust the salt as per your taste.

7. If you want this to be soupy, you might need to add more water and simmer some more.

8. Finish off with crushed peanuts and fresh cilantro.

9. Serve hot with rotis or alone.

Green Pea Curry with Brown Rice

This balancing vegetarian dish makes a lovely hot lunch, and its calming spice blend smells heavenly.

From an Ayurvedic Standpoint:

This lovely Green Pea Curry is highly beneficial in pacifying Vata and Kapha Dosha where stressful feelings need to be regulated, whether it's intense sorrow in Kapha or fear and restlessness in Vata. Making this lovely vegetarian dish is a lovely mindful act, particularly when combined with the meditative act of making Indian Dosas as an accompaniment, a recipe that can also be found in this book in the Indian Special section.

Servings: 4

Time to Prepare: 35 minutes

Ingredients:

- 300 ml coconut milk
- 330 g/2 cup green split peas (soaked overnight in water and rinsed well)
- 1½ liters water
- 1 tomato (diced)
- 2 onions (diced)
- 2 tbsp ghee
- 2½ tsp fennel seeds
- 3 garlic cloves, (chopped)
- 2 green chillies (seeded and chopped)
- ½ tbsp ginger (grated)
- ½ tsp turmeric (ground)
- 1 tbsp cilantro (ground)
- 1 tsp garam masala
- Sea salt to taste
- 6 curry leaves (or more to serve)

Instructions:

1. In a medium saucepan, bring the split peas and water to a boil over medium heat. Then reduce the heat to low and cover for 30 minutes, or until cooked.

2. Strain the peas and set them aside, reserving the liquid.

3. In a wide frying pan over medium heat, heat the ghee.

4. Add the onion, ginger, garlic, and chilli, and cook for 5–7 minutes or until the onion is golden.

5. Cook for 2–3 minutes after adding the turmeric, coriander, and fennel seeds.

6. Add the tomato and cook for 5 more minutes, or until the tomato softens.

7. Now add garam masala and curry leaves and cook for 1 more minute.

8. Add 250 ml (1 cup) of reserved pea liquid and bring to a boil. Add the cooked peas, then the coconut milk, and reheat.

9. Adjust the salt.

10. Garnish with curry leaves and serve alongside Indian dosas, roti, or rice.

RAITAS

Cucumber Raita

Cucumber Raita is a yogurt-based Indian side dish or dip made with fresh cucumbers, herbs, and spices. Cucumber Raita is a common side dish to serve with biryani, pulao, or any other Indian meal.

From an Ayurvedic Standpoint:

The skin of a cucumber is bitter, yet the inner part is cooling and sweet. Both the cucumber and the yogurt in this recipe are beneficial to Vata and Pitta, but when eaten in excess, they may trigger Kapha. Kapha can consume this occasionally, with additional hing and mustard seeds.

Servings: 4

Time to Prepare: 15 minutes

Ingredients:

- 2 cucumbers (peeled and grated)
- ½ cup plain yogurt
- 3 tbsp ghee
- ½ tsp black mustard seeds
- ½ tsp cumin seeds
- 4 curry leaves (fresh or dried)
- ½ small green chilli (chopped)
- 1 handful of cilantro leaves (chopped)
- 1 pinch cayenne
- 1 pinch of hing

Instructions:

1. In a saucepan over medium heat, heat the ghee and add the mustard seeds, cumin seeds, hing, and curry leaves. Cook for a few minutes, or until the seeds pop.

2. Add the cayenne or chilli powder and cilantro, stir, and remove from the heat.

3. In a bowl, mix the yogurt and grated cucumber.

4. Stir in the cooled spices to the yogurt mixture and serve.

Mint Raita

This nutritious and yummy dip can enhance the flavor of your dishes. Fresh mint leaves have a distinct scent and taste, as well as nutritional and health benefits.

From an Ayurvedic Standpoint:

Mint Raita is one of the healthiest raitas because it aids digestion and mitigates the effects of consuming spicy and oily foods. Vata and Kapha can enjoy this in moderation, while Pitta can consume it frequently!

Servings: 4

Time to Prepare: 15 minutes

Ingredients:

- 1¼ cups yogurt (plain)
- ¼ cup onion (finely chopped)
- ½ cup mint leaves (loosely packed)
- 2 tbsp coriander leaves (chopped)
- ½ tsp cumin powder (roasted)
- Salt to taste
- A pinch of black salt

Instructions:

1. In a grinder, mix ½ cup loosely packed mint leaves, 2 tbsp coriander leaves, 2 tbsp yogurt, and salt.

2. Grind it until it reaches the consistency of smooth cream.

3. Add the remaining yogurt.

4. Whip it until it has a flawless texture.

5. Add in the mint paste, ½ tsp roasted cumin powder, and a sprinkle of black salt. Mix them.

6. Add the onion and mix properly.

7. Mint Raita is ready to be served (with biriyani or rice, Mint Raita is like the icing on the cake).

Beetroot Raita

This Beetroot Raita combines freshly chopped beetroot with yogurt, spices, and seasonings to make a delectable side dish.

From an Ayurvedic Standpoint:

Beetroots have many health advantages. If eaten daily, they are beneficial to people with Kapha and Vata constitutions. Beets are better consumed steamed or cooked, as they become easier to digest and dosha balancing.

Servings: 3

Time to Prepare: 30 minutes

Ingredients:

- 1 medium raw beet
- 1 tbsp yogurt
- 2 cups water
- 1 tsp sugar
- 1 tsp ghee
- 1 tsp black mustard seeds
- 2-3 curry leaves
- 1 tsp cumin seeds
- A pinch of hing
- Rock salt to taste
- Freshly chopped coriander or mint leaves (for garnishing)

Instructions:

1. Bring two cups of water to boil in a pan, then steam the beets until soft.

2. After the beets have cooled, grate them. Mix the grated beets with yogurt along with the salt and sugar in a wide bowl.

3. Heat the ghee in another pan and add the mustard seeds. After the mustard seeds

have popped, add the curry leaves, cumin seeds, and hing to the ghee.

4. Turn off the heat and pour the ghee and spices over the yogurt and beet mixture, stirring well.

5. Garnish the raita with freshly chopped coriander (cilantro) or mint leaves if wanted.

Cucumber Dill Raita

This refreshing summer side dish goes well with curries and other hearty main dishes. This raita is packed with nutrients and made with a variety of Indian herbs, yogurt, and cucumber.

From an Ayurvedic Standpoint:

The skin of a cucumber is bitter, yet it is cooling and soft. The cucumber and yogurt in this recipe both help to reduce Vata Dosha. Yogurt has a binding quality (Grahi), making it useful as a supportive aid in diarrhea and dysentery. The health advantages of fresh yogurt include reduced bloating, relief from constipation and diarrhea, and relief from other gastrointestinal disorders. (Do you know that yogurt is the only "fermented" food that Ayurveda accepts as Sattvic.)

Servings: 4

Time to Prepare: 15 minutes

Ingredients:

- ½ cup yogurt (plain)
- 2 fresh medium cucumbers (peeled and grated)
- Handful cilantro leaves (chopped)
- 2 tbsp fresh dill or 1 tsp dried (chopped)
- 3 tbsp ghee
- 1 pinch hing
- 1 pinch cayenne
- ½ tsp black mustard seeds
- ½ tsp cumin seeds
- Coriander (for garnishing)

Instructions:

1. Heat mustard seeds in the ghee until they pop, then add cumin, hing, cilantro, and cayenne.

2. Turn off the heat and add yogurt, cucumber, dill, and spices. Mix well.

3. Serve with garnished coriander if desired.

Pumpkin Raita

Pumpkin Raita is easy to prepare and delightful to eat. It's a filling side dish for any Indian meal. I highly recommend you try this time-honored Pumpkin Raita recipe, which is ideal for the Fall.

From an Ayurvedic Standpoint:

This simple Pumpkin Raita is ideal for Vatas. Since Vata is drying, cooling, and light, you should eat oily, warming, or heavy foods like Pumpkin Raita. Pumpkins are a kind of winter squash with a sweet flavor that helps to balance the Vata Dosha.

Furthermore, they are high in Vitamin A and nutritional fibers, as well as minerals and amino acids, making this raita an excellent way to add these nutrients into your diet.

Servings: 4

Time to Prepare: 30 minutes

Ingredients:

- 1 medium-sized pumpkin (chopped)
- 2 cups of water
- 1 cup of yogurt
- Fresh cilantro or mint leaves (chopped)
- 2 tsp ghee
- ½ tsp cumin seeds (roasted and grounded)
- 4-5 fenugreek seeds
- ½ tsp hing
- 2-3 curry leaves
- Rock salt to taste
- Sugar (optional)

Instructions:

1. Bring the water in a pot to a boil and steam the chopped pumpkin until tender but not mushy.

2. Extract the cooked pumpkin from the water and grate or mash them. Add the yogurt to it and put it aside.

3. In a small pan heat the ghee and mustard seeds until they sizzle. Add fenugreek seeds and roast until they are dark brown.

4. Next, stir in the hing and curry leaves. Then, pour the ghee mixture into the yogurt and pumpkin and mix well. Season with salt to taste.

5. Garnish with fresh coriander leaves and serve alongside your meal.

Radish and Yogurt Raita

Raitas are an easy and striking Indian yogurt condiment. Radish and Yogurt Raita is a crunchy curd-based side dish seasoned with fragrant spices. It's quick and simple to make.

From an Ayurvedic Standpoint:

Radishes are a low-calorie food that may help in weight reduction since they increase fat metabolism. As a part of the mustard family, the peppery sharpness of radish strengthens the heart and warms the gut, making it ideal for Vata.

Servings: 6

Time to Prepare: 25 minutes

Ingredients:

- 2 cups raw radish (grated)
- ½ cup yellow onion (chopped)
- 2 cups yogurt
- 1 tbsp ghee
- 2 tbsp cilantro
- 1 tsp mustard seeds
- ¼ tsp red chillies
- ¼ tsp salt

- 2-3 curry leaves (optional)
- ⅛ tsp hing (optional)

Instructions:

1. Sauté 1 tsp mustard seed in 1 tbsp ghee for 30 seconds, or until mustard seeds start to pop.

2. Stir in 1 seeded, dried red chilli. Add optional spice mix of 2-3 curry leaves and ⅛ tsp hing. Fry for 10 more seconds.

3. Add the chopped onions and continue to fry on medium heat for 2 minutes, or until the onions become translucent.

4. Stir in the grated radish and cook until the raw scent goes away. Turn off the heat and set it aside to cool down.

5. Whisk the yogurt until it's smooth and free of lumps. Season with radish, cilantro, and salt to taste. Blend thoroughly.

6. Serve chilled with rice.

Bottle Gourd Raita

Bottle Gourd Raita is an easy, soothing, and savory condiment sauce made from bottle gourd and curd (yogurt). It's refreshing on the palate and goes well with pulao, biryani, or any Indian meal.

From an Ayurvedic Standpoint:

According to Ayurveda, bottle gourd has a sweet flavor, a cooling quality, and is beneficial for balancing the Pitta and Vata Dosha. It is a cardiac tonic, a taste enhancer (palatable), and a source of energy and strength for the tissues and dhatus. This dish is best served in the summer.

Servings: 4

Time to Prepare: 30 minutes

Ingredients:

- ½ cup green bottle gourd (washed, peeled, and grated)
- ½ cup water

- 1 cup yogurt (plain)
- 2 tsp of ghee
- ½ tsp roasted peanut powder (roast raw peanuts in a skillet for 10-15 minutes and grind to a medium-fine powder)
- ½ tsp black mustard seeds
- ½ tsp cumin seeds
- pinch of hing
- Rock salt to taste
- 1 tsp sugar (optional)
- 2-3 curry leaves (optional)
- Fresh cilantro or coriander leaves (chopped, for garnishing)

Instructions:

1. Boil the water in a pot, then add the grated bottle gourd and a pinch of salt. After 10-15 minutes, strain the water into a cup and set it aside.

2. Squeeze the grated cooked pulp with your hands to extract excess water after the bottle gourd has cooled.

3. Whisk the yogurt in a separate bowl and add the grated and squeezed bottle gourd. Blend it thoroughly.

4. In a separate small pan, heat the ghee on medium-low, then add the mustard seeds and allow them to splutter. Add the cumin seeds, curry leaves, and hing next. Turn off the heat.

5. While the yogurt is still hot, introduce the ghee and spice mixture over it. Season with salt and sugar to taste.

6. Add the roasted peanut powder and mix everything well.

7. Serve the raita garnished with fresh coriander.

Coconut Coriander Raita

This is a traditional South Indian dip that is both refreshing and tasty! It goes well with roasted vegetables, snacks, or rice. This irresistible mix of coconut, cilantro, lime juice, and red onion can quickly become a daily condiment in your kitchen.

It is fast and simple to prepare, and by using it in your meals, you can improve the digestibility of your food, encourage mild detoxification, and minimize inflammation. Excessive heat, liver weakness, skin disorders, heavy metal toxicity (great for chelation!), and allergies are some other general problems that this recipe can help with.

From an Ayurvedic Standpoint:

While primarily cooling, this chutney retains a hint of warmth and can be used all year to aid digestion, foster health, and make delightful meals! Vata and Pitta people can eat this raita often, while Kapha people should eat it in moderation.

Servings: 3

Time to Prepare: 10 minutes

Ingredients:

- 1 red onion (chopped)
- 1 cup coconut (sliced)
- ¼ cup coriander leaves
- 1 tsp lime juice
- Water (as needed)
- 1 green chilli
- Salt for taste

Instructions:

1. Add all the ingredients to a grinder and blend into a fine paste. Achieve your desired consistency by adding more or less water.

Chatpata Chana Raita (Garbanzo Raita)

Chatpata Chana Raita is not only a delicious side dish for any recipe, but it is also a perfect diet dish. If you eat a big bowl of it, you'll be satisfied both physically and mentally.

From an Ayurvedic Standpoint:

According to Ayurvedic principles, gram flour is calming to Pitta and Kapha due to its astringent flavor, but Vata types shouldn't overdo it. You can, however, make it even more balancing as a Vata food by incorporating spices and/or ghee, serving it moist, and with Vata-calming flavors including sweet, sour, and salty.

Servings: 5

Time to Prepare: 30 minutes

Ingredients:

- ½ cup shredded carrots (steamed for 3-4 minutes)
- 1 cup garbanzo beans/chickpea (cooked)
- 4 cups fresh yogurt
- 2 medium potatoes (boiled, peeled, and diced into cubes)
- 1 tbsp ghee
- ½ cup water
- ½ tsp ginger (minced)
- 1 tbsp fresh cilantro (chopped)
- ½ cup cashews (split)
- 2 tsp organic Vata Churna
- 1 tsp black or brown mustard seeds

Instructions:

1. Blend the cashew pieces and water to make a watery yet smooth paste.

2. Whisk in the yogurt, cashew paste, minced ginger, and organic Vata Churna.

3. Next, add in the garbanzos, potatoes, and carrots and mix thoroughly.

4. Heat the ghee and toss in the mustard seeds.

5. Turn off the heat as the seeds pop and pour the ghee and mustard seeds over the yogurt mixture.

6. Mix thoroughly. Garnish with fresh cilantro if desired.

CHUTNEYS

Tamarind Apple Chutney

This heartwarming side dish is an excellent, tasty topping for rice, quinoa, or any other whole grain thanks to the combination of sweet and sour notes with fall-inspired spices.

From an Ayurvedic Standpoint:

This chutney has many Ayurvedic benefits. Sweet, sour, and salty tastes complement Vata Dosha/Air energy. The combination of cleansing rock salt, sour tamarind paste, and sweet apples is ideal for a Vata side dish.

There are over 7500 apple varieties in the world. The majority of apples sold in supermarkets are crisp, slightly dry, and high in Air (Vata) energy. Cooked apple is ideal for Vata types, as it relieves bloating, anxiety, constipation, dryness, and menstrual irregularities.

Tamarind aids digestion and acts as a grounding agent for any bodily instabilities. Spasms, tremors, irregular digestion, and irregular menstruation are a few examples. It aids in the processing of bodily fluids, such as digestive enzymes and reproductive fluid.

Since cinnamon contains a lot of Fire energy, it's a great heating spice for warming up an imbalanced "Air" element and melting excess "Earth/Water" elements. It is excellent for maintaining blood sugar stability, dissolving extra fat, reducing headaches, lethargy, and anxiety.

Servings: 4

Time to Prepare: 30 minutes

Ingredients:

- 1 apple (peeled and diced)
- 1 cup water

- 1 tsp tamarind pulp
- 3 tsp cane sugar (unrefined)
- ¼ tsp clove powder
- ¼ tsp cinnamon powder
- Pinch of pink rock salt

Instructions:

1. Heat all the ingredients in a small pot over low-medium heat, with the lid slightly open to let out excess steam.

2. Cook for 30 minutes, or until the sauce has thickened somewhat and the apples are tender.

3. Serve as a delightful side dish with rice, dal, and cooked vegetables!

Cilantro Chutney

This is a basic recipe that makes use of the amazing coriander leaf (cilantro). It is not only tasty, but it is also a good way to start purifying heavy toxins (known as Garavisha) from the body. If you're a Vata type, you should definitely add Cilantro Chutney with holy basil (Tulsi) to your diet.

From an Ayurvedic Standpoint:

The dish is suitable for all three doshas. The cilantro is said to assist in the removal of heavy metals, while the holy basil aids in the elimination of two types of toxins known by Ayurveda—Amavisha and Garavisha. If you cultivate it in your house, it will also help to purify the air. In the fall, this is a great way to enjoy all the fresh cilantro!

Servings: 5

Time to Prepare: 10 minutes

Ingredients:

- 2 tsp maple syrup
- 1 bunch fresh cilantro (chopped)
- ½ cup dry coconut
- 1 tbsp lime juice

- ½ green chilli (no seeds)
- 2 cloves garlic
- ¼ tsp ginger (minced)
- ½ tsp salt
- 2-3 tbsp water (or more as per the desired consistency)

Instructions:

1. In a blender, blend chopped cilantro, garlic, ginger, salt, lemon, and chilli.

3. Then, add dry coconut and maple syrup and water as needed. Blend properly.

3. That's it! Serve with your main meal.

Vata Chutney

This chutney is more of an appetizer. Eating about 1 tsp of this mix 20-minutes before the main meal (lunch or dinner) can help Vata people with digestion. And of course, you can eat this as a condiment on the side with any meal.

From an Ayurvedic Standpoint:

People with Vata characteristics have dry skin, constipation, and anxiety. This is a sweet chutney that balances the Vata Dosha and aids digestion. It activates the digestive fire (Agni) and raises the life force (Prana), providing a sense of stability and vitality.

Servings: 6

Time to Prepare: 15 minutes

Ingredients:

- ½ cup raisins (pre-soaked in water)
- ½ cup orange juice (freshly squeezed)
- 1 cup dates (pitted)
- ½ tsp ground coriander
- ½ tsp fresh ginger toot (peeled)
- ½ tsp fennel seeds
- ½ tsp cumin seeds

Instructions:

1. Mix all ingredients into a food processor or blender until you get a semi-liquid consistency like jelly. If you don't have a food processor or blender, you can make use of the traditional stone blender (my grandma used to make chutneys with that).

Raisin Date Chutney

Packed with flavor and healthy spices, this Raisin Date Chutney is a perfect accompaniment to khichdi, grain dishes, and Indian snacks like samosa!

From an Ayurvedic Standpoint:

Raisin Date Chutney is perfect for autumn. Its sweet taste balances the Vata and Pitta Dosha that are prevalent during this season of transition.

Servings: 6

Time to Prepare: 15 minutes

Ingredients:

- 1 cup dates
- 1 cup raisins
- 1 tbsp orange juice
- 1 tbsp lime juice
- 1 tbsp fresh grated ginger
- 1 tsp fennel seed
- 1 tsp cumin seed
- ½ tsp coriander seed
- ½ tsp lime zest
- ½ tbsp jalapeno or more (to taste)
- ½ tsp salt

Instructions:

1. Soak the dates and raisins in water for 10 minutes.

2. Meanwhile, heat the spice seeds in a dry skillet until they release their scent. Take care not to burn them. Put aside.

3. After 10 minutes (when the dates and raisins are ready), in a food processor, mix the dates and raisins (drained) with the remaining ingredients and pulse to combine.

Serve instantly or refrigerate in a glass container for up to a week.

Nariyal Chutney (Coconut Chutney)

When it comes to South Indian cuisine, coconut is a common ingredient. Indeed, it is said to be ideal for most dishes, especially the damn coconut chutney.

From an Ayurvedic Standpoint:

This is tridosha balancing chutney known as Nariyal Chutney in Hindi. It is primarily Vata and Pitta calming.

The main ingredient, coconut, transforms the chutney into a total comfort snack. It's delicious with Dosa (thin rice flour and pulses pancake), Idli (steamed rice cakes), Uthapam (thick rice pancakes filled with veggies), and also as a sandwich spread. Overall, Nariyal Chutney is extremely helpful since it is cooling, increases vitality, and strengthens the body.

Servings: 4

Time to Prepare: 15 minutes

Ingredients:

- 2 tbsp cilantro
- 1 cup coconut flakes
- 1 tbsp ghee
- ¼-inch fresh ginger
- 1 tsp mustard seeds
- 2 pinch red chillies
- ¼ tsp curry leaves
- ¼ tsp hing

Instructions:

1. Roast the coconut until the scent gets strong but before it browns. Then using a food processor, grind the coconut, ginger, and cilantro into a fine paste with enough water to achieve the perfect consistency (about ¾ cup).

2. Heat the ghee and sauté the mustard seeds before they start popping. Cook for 15 seconds after adding the hing, curry leaves, and red chillies (before spices brown).

Stir in the coconut mixture.

3. Enjoy with your favorite South Indian dish.

Sesame Chutney

This is a simple chutney that adds a lot of flavor and texture to South Indian snacks. Sesame Chutney complements idlis, dosas, uthapam, and rice kanji.

From an Ayurvedic Standpoint:

This chutney is tridoshic, but it is particularly beneficial to those with Vata and Kapha imbalances. It is ideal for use as part of an Ayurvedic cleanse.

Servings: 4

Time to Prepare: 15 minutes

Ingredients:

- 1 cup fresh coconut (grated or desiccated)
- 3 tbsp roasted sesame seeds (in a pan roast them stirring often till they become a light golden)
- 2 tbsp roasted peanuts (in a pan roast them stirring often till they become crunchy)
- 3 dry red Kashmiri chillies or dry red Byadgi chillies (broken and de-seeded)
- 2 to 3 garlic cloves
- 1 tbsp tamarind (seedless)
- 1 cup water (or as required)
- Salt to taste

Instructions:

1. Add roasted peanuts, roasted sesame seeds, and fresh grated or desiccated coconut in a blender jar.

2. Next, add the tamarind, garlic cloves, and red chillies. As required, season with salt.

3. Finally, add 1 cup of water or as required to achieve the desired consistency.

4. Grind all the ingredients together to make a smooth paste.

5. Serve with idli, dosa, rice kanji, or other south Indian snacks such as uthapam, medu vada, etc.

Khajur Chutney (Date Chutney)

Dates are delicious on their own or with hot milk, but they also go well with most other ingredients. Dates make a tasty and quick chutney.

From an Ayurvedic Standpoint:

Dates (Khajur) are well-known for their Ayurvedic health benefits. These advantages have led to their widespread usage in medicines and therapies. Dates have Madhura Rasa (sweet), a quality that causes them to moisten the Dhatus (bodily tissues) in our bodies. They are cooling and help to stabilize the Vata and Pitta. They can help with arthritis, constipation, cystitis, acidity, anemia, and diarrhea.

Servings: 6

Time to Prepare: 15 minutes

Ingredients:

- 1 cup pitted dates (packed)
- ½ cup orange juice
- ¼ cup lemon juice
- ¼ tsp ground coriander
- ¼ tsp ground cardamom
- ⅛ tsp ground cloves
- 1 tbsp ghee
- ¼ tsp black mustard seeds
- ¼ tsp salt

Instructions:

1. In a saucepan, heat the ghee. Sauté the mustard seeds over low heat until they pop.

2. Add the remaining ingredients. Simmer for 10 minutes, covered.

3. Blend or process until smooth in a blender or food processor.

Fresh Mango Chutney

A fantastic chutney to enjoy with appetizers or as a side dish to your favorite foods.

From an Ayurvedic Standpoint:

Since this Mango Chutney includes a balance of sweet (Madhur) and sour (Amla) flavors, it instantly calms all Vata aspects–body and mind.

Servings: 4

Time to Prepare: 15 minutes

Ingredients:

- 3 cups medium raw mangoes (remove skin and seed and dice in cubes)
- 1 cup fresh cilantro (chopped)
- 2 cloves garlic
- 1 red chilli (cut off the head)
- 1 tsp salt (or more as per taste)

Instructions:

1. After preparing the ingredients, add them to a blender and blend until they reach a medium-coarse consistency.

2. Transfer to a serving dish and serve with appetizers or your favorite dish.

Poppy Seed Chutney

Apart from being tasty, this poppy seed chutney also acts as a natural sleep aid by calming Vata in the mind and Pitta in both the heart and the mind.

From an Ayurvedic Standpoint:

It helps to calm Vata, especially in the mind (Prana). It soothes Pitta in the heart and mind (Sadhaka). These are the two doshas that are most likely to obstruct good quality sleep. When these two are balanced, you are quiet and center, and you will easily fall asleep. For best results, Eat Poppy Seed Chutney at night, an hour before going to bed.

Servings: 2

Time to Prepare: 15 minutes

Ingredients:

- 1 tsp white poppy seeds
- 1 tsp coconut powder (freshly grated)
- Pinches of ground cumin and turmeric
- ½ tsp ghee
- Water as needed

Instructions:

1. Mix white poppy seeds and coconut powder in a mixing bowl.

2. When mixing, add small amounts of water to form a thick paste.

3. In a frying pan, heat the ghee until it becomes clear (cloudiness is gone).

4. Stir in the turmeric and cumin.

5. Turn off the heat immediately, simmer off until the color and smell change.

6. Stir in the poppy seed mixture and set aside for 5 minutes.

7. Season with salt to taste.

Coconut Mint Chutney

This goes well with idli, dosa, uttapam, pongal, and vada, but it can also be used as a spread on sandwiches, wraps, or rolls. It's a versatile chutney.

From an Ayurvedic Standpoint:

Coconut Mint Chutney is an excellent example of how Ayurvedic values can be used to even out prohibited ingredients.

Mint is a no-no for Vata since it dries and disperses. Pitta does not tolerate mustard seed since it is warming. Since coconut is heavy, it is forbidden to Kapha. Coconut Mint Chutney is a tasty tridoshic treat that is good for all three doshas when combined. Mint lightens coconut for Kapha. Mustard seed warms up the coconut for Vata and Kapha. For Pitta and Vata, coconut anchors the uplifting properties of mint and mustard seed.

Servings: 6

Time to Prepare: 10 minutes

Ingredients:

- 1 cup coconut flakes
- ¼ cup water
- ½ cup mint
- ½ tbsp lime juice
- 1 tsp mustard seeds
- ½ tsp sugar
- 2 pinches of salt

Instructions:

1. Roast the mustard seeds until they pop. Add all ingredients to a food processor and blend properly.

2. Enjoy with your favorite dish!

Khatti Meethi Imli Ki Chutney (Sour and Sweet Tamarind Chutney)

Sweet and Sour Tamarind Chutney, also known as Imli Ki Chutney (Sonth), is a tasty Indian sauce made with tamarind, jaggery, and spices. This simple chutney can be used to make Bhel Puri, served with samosas, and is an essential component of any Indian Chaat.

From an Ayurvedic Standpoint:

The sour flavor is juicy! According to the 14th chapter of Bhojana Kutuhalam, tamarind is very sour when unripe, and when completely ripened, it is sweet and sour, and it aids in the relief of constipation and Vata vitiation. This chutney, when mixed with spices, stimulates salivation, the stomach for digestion, and causes loose stools.

Servings: 120 ml

Time to Prepare: 30 minutes

Ingredients:

- ½ cup tamarind (deseeded)
- ½ cup jaggery
- ½ cup pitted dates (substitute with 3-4 tbsp jaggery)

- 2 cups water (or more if needed)
- ½ tsp ghee
- ½ tsp salt
- ¼ tsp garam masala (or ¾ tsp roasted coriander powder)
- ⅛ tsp hing
- ½ tsp red chilli powder
- ½ tsp fennel powder (roasted)
- ½ tsp cumin powder (roasted)
- ½ tsp ginger powder

Instructions:

1. Heat ½ tsp ghee in a pot. Add a pinch of hing to it.

2. Add water, tamarind, dates, and jaggery as well.

3. Bring all ingredients to a boil until the dates and tamarind are tender. If the mixture becomes too thick, add another half cup of water. Some dates and tamarind need more water.

4. Next, add the red chilli powder, salt, fennel powder, coriander powder, ginger powder, and cumin powder.

5. Mix all these ingredients and continue to cook for 2 to 3 minutes, or until the flavors of the spices emerge.

6. Allow the mixture to cool fully. Check if any tamarind or dates seeds are remaining in the pulp. Throw them out.

7. Pour the whole mixture into a blender jar and puree until smooth. (At this stage, you can add around half a cup of boiled and cooled water to make the mixture blend smoothly.)

8. Place a sieve or colander over a large bowl. Then pour the pureed dates and tamarind and pass through.

9. You will get a rich, creamy Tamarind Chutney. Serve immediately or put in a clean, moist-free glass bottle in the refrigerator for up to 6 weeks.

SWEETS

Almond Butter Stuffed Dates

These stuffed dates are the ideal sweet treat to have on hand in the freezer for those days when you want something sweet but still want to nourish yourself.

From an Ayurvedic Standpoint:

Fresh dates are a favorite of the Ayurvedic diet since they are Sattvic (promoting mental calm and contentment) and are considered to nourish Ojas (the essence of our immune system).

Dates are said to encourage general good health and digestion since they are high in antioxidants, potassium, magnesium, iron, Vitamin B6, and dietary fiber. They are used as medication in depleted plasma tissue (Rasa Dhatu) conditions since they are deeply nourishing to the tissues and immune system. Dates are often used to treat reduced libido or infertility, as well as to nourish and invigorate sexual reproductive tissues. They are also known to contain phytohormones that resemble oxytocin, the 'heart and well-being' hormone. But dates, although balancing for Vata and Pitta, should always be consumed in moderation by all, but particularly Kapha due to their heavy, sweet nature.

Servings: 2

Time to Prepare: 10 minutes

Ingredients:

- 4 whole dates (dried)
- 2 tbsp almond butter
- 1 pinch cinnamon

Instructions:

1. Split open the dates. Fill the pocket with a teaspoon of almond butter using a

spoon.

2. Garnish with cinnamon and serve!

Sweet Potato Pie

It is a traditional sweet Thanksgiving pie. This creamy Sweet Potato Pie is subtly spiced and slices beautifully!

From an Ayurvedic Standpoint:

This pie makes it simple for Vata people to focus on the season's need for sweet, warming, grounding, and easily digestible foods. It is an Ayurvedic triumph of culinary deliciousness combined with health-promoting goodness; so much so that our 2-year-old wants to consume it for breakfast!

Servings: 8

Time to Prepare: 120 minutes

Ingredients:

- ¼ cup buttermilk
- ½ cup almond milk
- 2 cup sweet potato
- ½ tsp cinnamon
- ⅓ cup sugar
- ¼ cup ghee
- ½ tsp nutmeg
- 1 tsp vanilla extract
- An unbaked oatmeal pie crust (can be found in any grocery store)

Instructions:

1. Boil the sweet potatoes with the skin on until tender (about 40 minutes)

2. Once the potato has cooled, remove the skins. Soaking them in cold water would enable them to cool faster.

3. Mash the potatoes and mix them with all the remaining ingredients.

4. Pour the filling into an unbaked oatmeal pie crust.

5. Bake for an hour at 350°C, or until a knife inserted into the middle comes out clean.

Sesame Seed Treats with Ginger and Ghee

This nutty morsel is rich and decadent on the tongue, with a delicious ginger zing. Don't be fooled by their tiny size; this tasty treat is strong and filling, making it an ideal small dessert or an energy-packed snack on the hiking trails.

From an Ayurvedic Standpoint:

Sesame increases body heat and blood circulation, particularly when combined with a warming, stimulating pinch of ginger. On a cold night, sesame combined with ginger can warm Vata people to their core. Many that are afraid of the bone-chilling weather drops that winter brings will find great solace in this healing dessert.

Servings: 4

Time to Prepare: 10 minutes

Ingredients:

- 2 tbsp sesame seeds
- 2 tbsp ghee
- ¼ tsp ginger
- 2 tsp sugar
- ¼ cup water
- Some almonds for garnishing (sliced)

Instructions:

1. Chill the ghee and sesame.

2. Add sugar and ¼ cup water in a small pot. Lessen the syrup to 1 tbsp.

3. Turn off the heat and stir in the remaining ingredients.

4. Thoroughly mix all ingredients and shape into tablespoon-sized balls. If the ghee is too soft, put the mixture in the freezer for 15 minutes before rolling it into balls.

5. Garnish with some sliced almonds and enjoy!

Kaju Katli

This classic sweet, Kaju Katli is one of the most bought sweets from the Halwai and Indian sweet shops during festivals and occasions. Most Indians usually gift these to friends and relatives to spread the joy of festive or special occasions.

Kaju translates to cashews, and Katli refers to a thin slice. These Kaju Katli have a smooth and melt-in-the-mouth texture with mild flavors of cardamom powder or rose water.

Often people are intimated to make Kaju Katli at home, as most recipes require checking the string consistency. But this recipe is very simple, quick to make, and does not involve checking string consistency.

From an Ayurvedic Standpoint:

Cashews are sweet and heavy, and they can relax your nerves as well as satisfy your stomach. The crescent-shaped cashew is dense and warm, boosting strength and keeping you feeling nourished, particularly during the cooler months. With each bite, these crunchy nuts turn creamy and smooth. Cashews may be used to fulfill your crunchy cravings by sprinkling them on top of curries, adding them to stir-frys, or crumbling them on top of your morning oatmeal. Cashews have one of the smoothest textures of any nut and can be used to make a creamy nut butter spread, silky homemade cashew milk, or soft cashew cheeses.

These nuts are native to Brazil and are technically the seeds of the cashew apple. You'll understand why cashews are some of the costliest nuts on supermarket shelves if you see how they're grown. From the bottom of each apple, a single cashew sprout. It is encased in a membrane that produces a poisonous residue, and must also be washed before eating. Since cashews are related to poison ivy, certain people are very allergic to them. They balance Vata and Pitta but are too heavy and difficult to digest for Kaphas.

Servings: 40 pieces

Time to Prepare: 20 minutes

Ingredients:

- 2 cup Kaju/cashew
- 1 cup sugar
- ½ cup water
- 1 tsp ghee

- ¼ tsp cardamom powder

Instructions:

1. To begin, in a mixer, add 2 cups of cashews and blend to a fine powder. If you don't pulse and blend, the cashews can release oil and turn into a paste.

2. Sieve the cashew powder to remove any lumps. Keep it aside.

3. Add ½ cup sugar and ½ cup water in a big kadhai.

4. Dissolve the sugar well by stirring. Boil for 5 minutes, or until the 1 string consistency is reached.

5. Stir in the powdered cashews.

6. Continue to stir until the mixture is well mixed and forms a smooth paste.

7. Stir in ¼ tsp cardamom powder and 1 tsp ghee. Mix thoroughly.

8. Cook until the mixture becomes a thick paste and begins to separate slightly from the Kadhai. (If you overcook the burfi, it will become hard.)

9. Spread the mixture out on the butter paper. Ghee can be used to grease the butter paper.

10. Fold the mixture with a spatula until it thickens and forms a dough.

11. After the dough has been formed, knead it gently to make a smooth dough. Place this cashew dough between butter paper and roll using a rolling pin.

12. Roll it out slightly thick and even.

13. Grease with ghee and add silver leaf or silver vark (optional)

14 Cut into a diamond form or any shape of your choice.

15. That's it! When stored in an airtight container, these heavenly Kaju Katli would last for a month.

Rice pudding with Raisins and Cinnamon

Rich, creamy Rice Pudding with a hint of vanilla and cinnamon and juicy raisins. This is the perfect comfort meal!

From an Ayurvedic Standpoint:

Rice pudding with Raisins and Cinnamon is a tasty dessert that is simple and convenient to prepare since the rice can be cooked in advance. Many who practice Ayurveda would know that it is beneficial to all three doshas. Cinnamon is an excellent pacifier of Vata and Kapha Dosha, and raisin helps in improving Vata's excretion process and abdominal functions.

Servings: 4

Time to Prepare: 10 minutes

Ingredients:

- ⅓ cup basmati rice
- 2 cup milk
- ⅓ cup raisins
- 1 tsp vanilla extract
- ¼ cup raw sugar
- ¼ tsp cinnamon
- 2 pinch salt

Instructions:

1. Mix all the ingredients in a single pot.

2. Bring to a boil while continuously stirring to keep the rice and milk from sticking to the bottom of the pot.

3. Reduce the heat to a simmer. Stir regularly until the rice softens and thickens.

4. Keep it covered. Serve.

Banana with Ghee and Cinnamon

Simply heat some ghee, toss in some bananas, and watch them sizzle whenever you're hungry. These morsels are made even more tasty with a dash of spices, such as cinnamon and ginger. This hearty, nourishing snack couldn't be simpler to prepare or more filling from the inside out. It's perfect for a quick snack, a light breakfast, or a healthy dessert.

From an Ayurvedic Standpoint:

Bananas in sizzling ghee are filling, hearty, and Ojas-inducing. They're perfect for autumn, when the body craves sweet, fatty foods to prepare for winter. As fall approaches, warm sweaters, richer foods, and cozy evenings offer comfort from the cooler temperatures and anxiety of a busy fall schedule.

Servings: 1

Time to Prepare: 10 minutes

Ingredients:

- 1 cup banana (peeled and diced in small pieces)
- 2 pinch cinnamon
- 1 tsp ghee
- 2 pinch ginger (dried)
- Some cardamom for garnishing

Instructions:

1. Deep fry the bananas in ghee for the best results. Otherwise, dice the bananas and sauté them in ghee, tossing gently to avoid mushing.

2. Garnish with spices like cardamom and cinnamon.

Baked Apple with Rosemary

As autumn approaches, the summer's ripe peaches, mangos, and berries fade, allowing one fruit to glow brightly: apples. Starting the day with a stewed apple can help promote regular bowel movements, improve stamina and alertness, and provide a light yet rewarding start to the day.

From an Ayurvedic Standpoint:

The crunch and astringency of apples will aggravate Vata Dosha, which is naturally dry, light, and cool, so it's no surprise that apples are often cooked in autumn recipes. Cooking helps us to soothe Vata with a warm, sweet dish that is ideal for breakfast or as a snack.

Servings: 4

Time to Prepare: 40 minutes

Ingredients:

- 4 cups apple
- 2 tsp rosemary
- ¼ cup ghee
- ½ tsp cardamom

Instructions:

1. Preheat the oven to 375°F.

2. Wash the apples, split them in half, remove the core, and place them face down in a baking dish.

3. In a saucepan, melt the ghee and drizzle it uniformly over the apples, or brush each one with a light coat.

4. Evenly sprinkle with fresh rosemary and cardamom. Place in the oven and bake for 40 minutes, or until the potatoes are soft. Serve warm.

Coconut Butter

Coconut Butter is a deliciously creamy whole food produced from dried coconut flesh. This delightful tropical treat melts in your mouth. Warm it up before using it as a spread.

From an Ayurvedic Standpoint:

The coconut is a sensory and physical treat, and it is the very sign of tropical paradise. This idyllic and pleasant tree nut preserves equilibrium and peace. It is light and sweet, calming to the skin and nerves, and nourishing while stimulating energy.

Servings: 20

Time to Prepare: 20 minutes

Ingredients:

- 4 cups coconut flakes

Instructions:

1. Puree 4 cups of coconut flakes in a blender on high for 8 minutes, pushing down the sides as you go.

2. The coconut flakes will undergo 3 stages in the transformation to coconut butter. First, the flakes will be finely ground. Second, the texture will become a grainy liquid. Finally, it will become a smooth, thick liquid. The final texture will ultimately be thick, slightly grainy peanut butter.

3. Pour the coconut butter into a jar and use it appropriately!

Almond Coconut Fudge

Almond Coconut Fudge is a smooth and creamy treat. When it melts in your mouth, you'll find that the nourishing coconut oil soothes cravings as deep as your body's cells. Consider yourself on a sunny beach, with the scent of salt and coconut in the air. Almond Coconut Fudge is like a 5-minute holiday that revitalizes you from the inside out.

From an Ayurvedic Standpoint:

Your body craves fatty foods in the fall as it prepares to create a layer of insulating fats for winter defense. In the fall, Vata types need heartier foods and can experience an overwhelming need for fats and sweet treats. At this time of year, it's important to feed your body healthy fats, which will nourish and relax your nervous system, shield your body from colds and flu later in the season, and provide the fuel you'll need to stay warm.

Servings: 2

Time to Prepare: 10 minutes

Ingredients:

- ¼ cup almond butter
- 1 tbsp honey
- 1 tbsp ghee
- ¼ tsp cinnamon
- ¼ tsp dried ginger (powdered)
- 1 pinch salt
- Ground cacao (for crunch)

Instructions:

1. In a bowl, mix all the ingredients and mash them together until thoroughly com-

bined. The fudge will harden in the refrigerator or remain soft at room temperature.

2. For a chocolatey crunch, try adding ground cacao.

Masala Gud (Spicy Jaggery Bites)

Masala Gud, also known as Spicy Jaggery Bites, is an iron-rich winter special sweet and a tasty digestive treat made from all nutritious and delicious ingredients.

From an Ayurvedic Standpoint:

Jaggery provides more calories than many other sweeteners and has numerous healing properties. It not only balances Vata, but it also assists metabolism, flushes off toxins, boosts immunity, and also eases menstrual pains! It is rich in vitamins, zinc, selenium, potassium, magnesium, iron, and other essential nutrients, making it much superior to white sugar. It's still much healthier than raw honey, maple syrup, and most dried fruit so it's inexpensive to use as your daily sweetener as well.

Servings: 5

Time to Prepare: 25 minutes

Ingredients:

- 500 gm Jaggery (crushed or grated)
- 2 tbsp ghee
- 2 tbsp desiccated coconut
- 15 pieces almond
- 1 tbsp onion seeds
- 2 tbsp fennel seeds
- 1 tbsp sesame seeds
- 1 tbsp coriander seeds
- 1 tsp black pepper
- ½ tbsp dry ginger powder
- 5-6 green cardamom

Instructions:

1. Grease and set aside a plate or a square dish.

2. Dry roast all the ingredients except dry ginger powder on slow heat.

3. Lightly crush the black pepper, green cardamom, and coriander seeds in a mortar and pestle or with a rolling pin.

4. Break up the almond seeds into little bits.

5. Heat the ghee in a thick-bottomed pan over low to medium heat.

6. When the ghee has warmed, add the crushed/grated jaggery.

7. Allow the jaggery to melt slowly, stirring occasionally, so that it does not stick to the bottom of the pan.

8. Once the jaggery has melted, add the ginger powder. Mix thoroughly.

9. Now add and mix in all the remaining ingredients.

10. Pour the mixture onto the greased plate as rapidly as possible.

11. Using the back of a spoon or a spatula, gently move to spread and form an even sheet.

12. Allow it to cool for a few minutes. Give it the desired shape. This must be achieved when it is still somewhat warm, or it would be difficult to cut.

13. Allow to cool fully before storing in an airtight jar.

Shrikhand (Yogurt Cheese with Pistachios, Sugar, and Saffron)

Sweet and creamy Shrikhand made from luscious Greek yogurt with crushed nuts, a touch of cardamom for taste, and saffron for that dark golden glow, with as much or as little sugar as you want, makes for a tasty instant dessert.

From an Ayurvedic Standpoint:

Fresh homemade yogurt is considered Pitta and Vata friendly. This is because new homemade yogurt is not sour. It gets sour and ferments as it ages, rendering it unsuitable for Pittas. For all practical purposes, Greek yogurt is the same as traditional store-bought yogurt, just smoother and less bitter. As a result, it is Kapha aggravating and mildly Pitta aggravating. Saffron is tridoshic, pacifies Vata, and is excellent for blood purification, acne reduction, and skin and eye health. Cardamom is tridoshic and aids digestion.

Servings: 4

Time to Prepare: 10 minutes

Ingredients:

- ¼ cup pistachios
- 4 cup homemade yogurt
- 1 tbsp milk
- ¼ tsp cardamom
- 2 pinch nutmeg
- 1 cup sugar
- 2 pinches of saffron
- Some rose petals for garnishing (optional)

Instructions:

1. Drain the liquid from the yogurt by wrapping it in cheesecloth and hanging it from the kitchen faucet overnight.

2. Using a mortar and pestle, grind the saffron.

3. Fill the mortar with 1 tbsp warm milk and soak the saffron powder for 10 minutes. Chop pistachios.

4. Mix all ingredients and put in muffin tins.

5. Chill and turn over. Garnish with rose petals if desired.

Lapsi (Cracked Wheat Sweet)

Sweet Lapsi or Cracked Wheat Sweet is a simple three-ingredient dessert that is both tasty and healthier than other Indian sweets since it does not use refined sugar to sweeten it. It is traditionally prepared on auspicious days such as Graha Pravesh (the first day in a new house), Diwali, Dusherra, and Navratri, with the first morsel given to the gods and goddesses.

From an Ayurvedic Standpoint:

Wheat helps to balance Vata by offering warmth, heaviness, and softness. Cooked whole grain contains both of these properties. Aside from its role in Vata balancing, grain has a plethora of other beneficial properties. It is Sattvic in nature, which means it promotes balance and harmony.

Servings: 5

Time to Prepare: 25 minutes

Ingredients:

- ½ cup Lapsi Dalia/cracked wheat
- ½ cups hot water
- ¼ cup ghee
- ½ cup jaggery (grated)
- ¼ tsp cardamom powder
- pinch of saffron strands
- Fistful of sliced nuts like almonds pistachios (optional)

Instructions:

1. Heat ghee in a nonstick pan over medium-low heat.

2. Once warm, add the Lapsi Dalia and sauté for 2-3 minutes, or until it turns dark brown and has a nutty aroma.

3. Reduce the heat to low and add the water, stirring constantly for 20 seconds.

4. Stir in the saffron. Allow Lapsi to cook for 5-8 minutes, or until the water has evaporated and Lapsi begins to leave the sides of the pan and ghee begins to ooze out.

5. Stir in the grated jaggery and mix until it is fully melted.

6. Add cardamom and cook for 2 -3minutes until dry.

7 Switch off the heat and garnish with the sliced nuts.

Baked Pear with Cardamom

The delicious taste of pear and the calming aroma of cardamom combine to create a quick breakfast or a stimulating mid-day snack. Baking the pears softens them and enhances their flavor.

From an Ayurvedic Standpoint:

Pear is high in "Air" energy, making it ideal for juggling excess Earth and Fire dosha, which Pitta and Kapha types commonly encounter. A ripened pear, on the other hand, is sweeter and has more Earth energy, making it ideal for Pitta people. Baked

Pears are good liver and blood cleansers for Vata types. They aid in the dissolution of congestion in the lungs and blood vessels. They can help with acne, inflammation, and heaviness in the body, as well as alleviate heavy menstrual cycles.

Servings: 2

Time to Prepare: 15 minutes

Ingredients:

- 2 whole pears
- ½ cup water
- ½ tsp cardamom

Instructions:

1. Preheat the oven to 350 ° F.

2. Place the pears in a baking dish.

3. Coat the dish's bottom with water.

4. Sprinkle cardamom on top of the pears.

5. Bake at 350°F until the pears get soft.

Gajar Ka Halwa (Indian Carrot Pudding)

The arrival of winter implies one thing in any Indian household: lots and lots of Gajar Ka Halwa. Gajar Ka Halwa, also known as Gajrela, is a Diwali-themed Indian carrot pudding. It goes well with a cup of Masala Chai.

From an Ayurvedic Standpoint:

Gajar Ka Halwa is a popular Ayurvedic carrot dessert that helps to balance the Vata Dosha. Carrots that have been cooked have a pleasant flavor and hot potency. Aside from the flavor, there are numerous reasons for us to consume this dessert. Carrots, for example, complement both the Vata and Kapha Dosha, have an Ushna (hot) potency that keeps you warm in the winter, improve the heart muscles, aid with Irritable bowel syndrome, raise Ojas (immunity), and a variety of other benefits.

The sweet flavor nourishes, grounds, and soothes the body, mind, and sense organs. It enhances the capacity and vitality of the 7 Dhatus (bodily tissues). An overdose of sweet flavor, on the other hand, may trigger lethargy, obesity, diabetes, swelling, and other negative effects.

Servings: 4

Time to Prepare: 45 minutes

Ingredients:

- 4 cups organic carrots (peeled and shredded)
- ½ cup cashews (chopped)
- ½ cup raisins
- 1½ cups organic whole milk
- 2 tbsp ghee, divided (1 tbsp and 1 tbsp)
- ½ tsp cardamom powder
- 5 tbsp sugar
- 1 tbsp pistachios for garnish (chopped)

Instructions:

1. Heat the ghee in a wok over medium heat.

2. Add the carrots and sauté for around 8 minutes, or until the color changes.

3. Continue stirring to prevent burning.

4. Pour the milk over the carrots. Cook the carrots and milk for 6-7 minutes, or until the carrots have consumed all the milk.

5. Continue to stir to prevent sticking and burning.

6. Stir in the sugar.

7. Immediately after that, add 1 tbsp more ghee.

8. Continue to stir until all the water left behind by the sugar is absorbed. This would take about 5-6 minutes.

9. When done, sprinkle with cardamom powder. Stir well.

10. Stir in the cashews and raisins. You may even include almonds or pistachios. Mix thoroughly.

11. Continue to dry roast the Gajar Ka Halwa for a few minutes more or until the color of the carrots deepens significantly.

12. Serve warm alongside masala tea.

Kheer (Rice Pudding)

Nothing can take place of a Kheer when it comes to a celebration in Indian Culture. You can say it is the national dessert of the country. And there's a reason for that—Kheer is the quintessential Indian dessert that every Indian grows up eating because it's made with simple ingredients that are readily available in homes.

Flavored with cardamom, nuts, and ghee, it's the best way to finish off an Indian meal.

From an Ayurvedic Standpoint:

This is a warm winter dessert that helps to stabilize Vata while still keeping Pitta healthy and balanced. Kheer or Rice Pudding stimulates the appetite and is easy to digest. This is an excellent source of carbs and calcium. This Ayurvedic recipe is simple to make and uses natural ingredients that are extremely helpful to your optimal health. However, if you are Kapha, you must be mindful of the quantity and frequency.

Servings: 2

Time to Prepare: 30 minutes

Ingredients:

- ¼ cup basmati rice
- 2 cups milk
- 2 cups water
- ⅓ cup sugar
- 1 tbsp ghee
- ½ tsp cardamom powder
- 10 cashews (chopped)
- 10 pistachios (chopped)
- 2 tbsp raisins

Instructions:

1. Wash the rice 3 times and completely drain it.

2. Bring the milk to a boil in a large pot.

3. Cook rice in water until nearly all the water has been absorbed, then add boiled milk in 2-3 parts. Cook the rice until it is tender and well cooked. If necessary, add more water or milk.

4. Continue to stir to stop letting the milk burn at the bottom.

5. Add the sugar and continue to cook until the Kheer thickens.

6. Add the cardamom powder and cook for another 5 minutes.

7. Roast the nuts and raisins in ghee in a separate pan. If necessary, fry the nuts and raisins in ghee. When the Kheer has reached the perfect consistency (slightly runny), add three-quarters of the roasted nuts and raisins with ghee to the Kheer, blend well, and turn off the heat.

8. It thickens after it has been set aside to cool. Garnish with any leftover roasted nuts, raisins, or ghee.

9. Eat the Kheer warm. It's still yummy when cooled down as well, however, it's better to consume warm for Vata for winter.

BEVERAGES

Warming Vata Tea

Is the cold winter making you sleepy and/or fatigued, forgetful, confused, nervous, or constipated? With this relaxing and calming Warming Vata Tea, you will balance the qualities of accumulated or aggravated Vata in your mind and body.

From an Ayurvedic Standpoint:

If your digestion is slow, heavy, or cold, drink this tea to boost it. The ginger's warming, light, and pungency can aid digestion. Cardamom promotes a downward energy flow. And Ajwain has a powerful influence on the Vata and Kapha Dosha, as well as a Pitta-calming effect on the body. This mixture is ideal for improving digestion.

Servings: 1

Time to Prepare: 10 minutes

Ingredients:

- 1 cup boiling water
- ¼ tsp ginger (fresh grated)
- ¼ tsp cardamom (ground)
- ¼ tsp cinnamon
- ¼ tsp ajwain/carom seeds (can be found online or at Indian grocery stores. If you cannot find ajwain seeds, they can be omitted from the recipe)

Instructions:

1. In a pot, bring the water to a boil.

2. Once hot, add the grated ginger, cardamom, cinnamon, and ajwain seeds.

3. Steep the tea for 5 minutes, covered.

4. Strain the herbs and spices out and serve warm.

Cumin, Coriander, and Fennel Tea

A medicinal and earthy herbal tea with a long history of usage in Ayurveda that is helpful to the digestive tract by eliminating gas and bloating.

From an Ayurvedic Standpoint:

The spices in this tea blend have sweet, salty, pungent, and bitter flavors, as well as corresponding moistening, drying, hot, and cold energetics, which have the net effect of balancing all three doshas.

This trio is used in Ayurvedic medicine to softly stoke the digestive fire, known as Agni, but not to the point of overheating. When the intestinal fire is in fantastic health, the body is better able to consume and use nutrients from food, as well as efficiently break down Ama, or stored toxins.

Servings: 1

Time to Prepare: 10 minutes

Ingredients:

- 1½ cup water
- ¼ tsp coriander seeds
- ¼ tsp cumin seeds
- ¼ tsp fennel seeds

Instructions:

1. Bring 1½ cups of water to a boil.
2. Stir in the cumin, coriander, and fennel seeds whole.
3. Allow to steep for 5 minutes, or until it has cooled to a drinkable temperature.
4. Strain and discard the spices before serving.

Gold Milk

People in South Asia regard milk as sacred since it (along with fruits) is one of the few foods that can be given freely without causing harm to the plant or animal. With devotion, a mother openly offers milk to a calf. As a result, gold milk is a nourishing and grounding drink that is a delightful way to finish the day.

From an Ayurvedic Standpoint:

Golden milk is excellent for soothing the Vata Dosha, which may become unbalanced during the winter and fall months. This nourishing tonic, however, can be consumed at any time of year! This drink recipe is both soothing and therapeutic for the mind and body.

Turmeric has balancing properties for all three doshas: its fire balances Vata and Kapha, its dryness and pungent and bitter flavors balance Kapha, and its bitter taste balances Pitta, making it tridoshic!

Servings: 1

Time to Prepare: 10 minutes

Ingredients:

- 1 cup milk
- 1 tsp honey
- 2 pinch cardamom
- 2 pinch cinnamon
- 2 pinch turmeric

Instructions:

1. Heat the milk with spices in a pan to a boil.

2. Turn off the heat.

3. Set aside for a few minutes to cool before pouring into a cup with honey (make sure the honey isn't heated together with the milk and herbs. Although honey can liquefy in warm milk, it is not advised to heat honey).

Badam Chai (Almond Milk Tea)

Badam Chai is produced by boiling almond milk until it releases the aroma. It's heavenly when it's made right.

From an Ayurvedic Standpoint:

With its warming, soothing, and relaxing Ayurvedic ingredients, use this Badam

Chai to regulate both excess "Air" and "Earth" in the body. This Badam Chai is ideal for Vata types in the autumn (the "Air") and winter (the "Earth") seasons, as it will help to calm the digestion and mind. It boosts your energy while also grounding you and holding you calmer, less nervous, and more relaxed!

Servings: 1

Time to Prepare: 15 minutes

Ingredients:

- ½ cup almond milk (if using unsweetened, add 1 tsp liquid sweetener to tea once finished cooking)
- 1 cup water
- ½ tsp cinnamon
- ¼ tsp nutmeg
- ¼ tsp cardamom
- 1-inch fresh ginger (peeled and chopped)
- 2 cloves

Instructions:

1. In a medium saucepan, add all ingredients except the cardamom and almond milk. Bring to a boil and stir until the spices are fully dissolved.

2. Cook until the water has been decreased to around half its original volume.

3. Reduce the heat to low-medium and add the almond milk. Cook for another 5 minutes.

4. Add in cardamom powder, and cook for 30 seconds. Turn off the heat and discard the cloves.

5. Enjoy any time of the day as an energy refresher!

Lemon and Spice Weight Loss Tea

Lemon and Spice Weight Loss Tea combines energizing cayenne with zesty lemon for a tea that's full of vigor.

From an Ayurvedic Standpoint:

This is a traditional, energetic Ayurvedic mixture for fat digestion and metabolism. A warm sensation deep in your abdomen can confirm these symptoms after consuming Lemon and Spice tea.

This hot Lemon and Spice Tea will brighten your cloudy morning mind and warm you up from head to toe with just one sip. Your senses are awakened by the sour lemon and apple cider vinegar. Cayenne pepper, with its bright, pungent flavor, can fire you up from the inside out. This tea becomes a metabolic lift that makes you feel great if you add a little honey for sweetness and also scrape fat and toxins.

Servings: 1

Time to Prepare: 10 minutes

Ingredients:

- 10 drops apple cider vinegar
- 1 cup water
- 1 tsp honey
- 1 pinch cayenne powder
- 1 tbsp lemon juice

Instructions:

1. Squeeze lemon and add remaining ingredients into hot water and stir.

2. Then add apple cider vinegar (you may use any type of vinegar, although I prefer apple cider vinegar for taste).

3. Serve warm.

Yogurt with Honey and Cinnamon

This naturally tasty snack will satisfy your sweet tooth. In a delicious medley with great poise, this simple dish combines the soft sweetness of honey, the rich savor of Greek yogurt, and the earthiness of roasted nuts.

From an Ayurvedic Standpoint:

Honey is an astringent that is drying. Cinnamon and cardamom are sharp pungent spices that break up some of the yogurt's moist qualities. Cloves boost circulation and push heat to the surface of the body. For Vata types, the combination of all these ingredients is extremely balancing.

Servings: 1

Time to Prepare: 10 minutes

Ingredients:

- ⅓ cup yogurt
- ⅔ cups water
- 1 tsp honey
- 2 pinch cardamom
- 2 pinch cinnamon
- 2 pinch cloves

Instructions:

1. Grind all the spices or use powdered. Puree all ingredients in a blender and serve.

Ayurvedic Breakfast Drink

If you had a heavy dinner the night before or are feeling tired, this morning drink made with almonds, dates, and cardamom is an excellent pick.

From an Ayurvedic Standpoint:

Calcium and magnesium are abundant in sweet almonds. Almonds are high in antioxidant factors, which help to reduce cholesterol. Almonds are classified as Vatama in Ayurveda, which implies they will calm the vitiated Vata Dosha. Dates' Balya (strength provider) property can also help to improve the nervous system. It often nourishes the nerves, which become dry as a result of an imbalanced Vata Dosha. This is due to its balancing Snigdha (oily) and Vata properties.

Servings: 1

Time to Prepare: 20 minutes

Ingredients:

- 8-10 whole almonds (soaked and peeled)
- 1 cup milk
- 3 medium-sized dates
- Pinch of cardamom powder (made by grinding the seeds of one green cardamom pod)
- Few strands of saffron (optional)

Instructions:

1. Add the almonds, dates, and milk to a blender.

3. Blend, then add in the saffron water and strands (if using) as well as the ground cardamom and serve. (If using saffron, soak for 10 minutes in 1 tbsp hot water before using.)

Mango Juice with Ghee, Cardamom, and Saffron

This traditional Indian drink, which has been cherished and appreciated by generations of Indians, is ideal for the summer. I can't praise this juice enough, but I'll suggest everyone must try this once, especially during summer.

From an Ayurvedic Standpoint:

Mangoes are nice and delicious, as well as cooling, nourishing, and Vata-balancing. Mango juice is Vata-soothing, tonic, heavy, laxative, and tonic. It lacks the heart tonic properties of other mango varieties and appears to raise Kapha, but it is nourishing and building.

Servings: 1

Time to Prepare: 15 minutes

Ingredients:

- 1 cup ripened mango (peeled and chopped)
- 1 pinch cardamom
- 1 tsp ghee
- 1 pinch saffron
- ½ cup water

Instructions:

1. Crush the saffron in a mortar and pestle after heating it in a plate over boiling water. Then, add freshly ground cardamom.

2. Warm the milk and add to the mortar and pestle to brew the saffron and cardamom.

3. Add all the ingredients in a blender with the mangoes and mix until smooth.

4. Pour into a glass and top with 1 tsp ghee. The liquid should be hot enough for the ghee to melt.

5. Serve at room temperature or chilled.

Butter Coffee

Butter Coffee is a drink made with brewed coffee, unsalted butter, and medium-chain triglycerides (MCTs), a type of fat that is easily digested. Butter Coffee can be consumed in place of breakfast by those following a keto diet, which is high in fat and low in carbs.

From an Ayurvedic Standpoint:

Coffee is both calming and depleting, but incorporating butter or ghee will help counteract the negative impact. Stable, nutritious saturated fats like those found in grass-fed butter and nourishing ghee calm your nerves and shield your stomach lining from acidic coffee.

Coffee is high in antioxidants, but it's still a powerful stimulant, so it's only prescribed on rare occasions in Ayurveda.

Butter Coffee is one of the few ways that Vata-types can enjoy a cup of coffee without being too stressed or exhausted. Vitamin A is abundant in grass-fed, organic butter (the yellow kind). Vitamin A is important for adrenal and thyroid health.

Servings: 1

Time to Prepare: 10 minutes

Ingredients:

- 2 tsp organic butter (unsalted)
- 1 tbsp coffee
- 2 tsp ghee
- ¼ tsp cardamom

Instructions:

1. Use the coffee grounds to brew a fresh batch of coffee and pour 1½ cup into a glass blender.

2. Blend in the ghee, butter, and cardamom until smooth.

3. Serve warm.

Chaas (Traditional Ayurvedic Buttermilk)

Buttermilk is a probiotic powerhouse! It's light, simple to digest, and has anti-inflammatory effects. This is a famous summer beverage in India, and it's made with yogurt. It's produced all over India, with slight regional differences.

From an Ayurvedic Standpoint:

It balances all three doshas, according to Ayurveda: Vata, Pitta, and Kapha. It's best to drink it after lunch to get the most benefits out of it.

Servings: 2

Time to Prepare: 10 minutes

Ingredients:

- 1 cup fresh yogurt
- 2 cup water
- ½ tsp roasted cumin powder
- ¼ tsp black salt powder (or more as per taste)
- Few coriander leaves or mint leaves for garnishing

Instructions:

1. In a blender jar, add all the above ingredients, excluding the coriander leaves.
2. Blend for a few seconds, or until everything is thoroughly blended and the mixture is frothy.
3. Pour it in a glass.
4. Serve immediately with coriander or mint leaves as a garnish.

Spiced Milk and Honey

This Spiced Milk and Honey restores a warm, nurturing glow that seems to emanate from your chest, much like a cozy fire. I recommend trying this recipe for deep and restful sleep. It induces restful slumbers by being both soothing and quickly digestible.

From an Ayurvedic Standpoint:

This Spiced Milk for sleep is tasty and warming, and it's the ideal way to cleanse your body of toxins while sliding you to sleep. This recipe contains some of our favorite superfoods, such as turmeric, ginger, honey, and cardamom, which are much easier to digest when mixed with healthy raw fat (like coconut milk/ghee).

A mug of warm spiced milk and honey not only soothes your nerves, it strengthens your whole constitution. In Ayurvedic terms, that means milk nourishes your ojas. This drink is especially useful in autumn for depleted Vata individuals with exhaustion, a cold feeling in the chest and persistent cough.

Servings: 1

Time to Prepare: 15 minutes

Ingredients:

- 1 tsp honey
- 1 cup milk
- ¾ tsp black pepper
- ¾ tsp cardamom
- ¾ tsp ginger (dried)
- 1 pinch cinnamon
- 1 pinch star anise
- 1 bay leaf

Instructions:

1. Bring milk to medium heat, then reduce to low heat and stir in all spices.

2. Cook, stirring frequently, for 5 minutes.

3. If the milk begins to foam, reduce the heat rapidly or turn off the heat. When milk gets too hot, it quickly boils over the side of the pan. It should have a shiny surface with small bubbles.

2. Remove from heat and drizzle with honey.

Peach Rosewater Lassi with Cardamom

The Peach Rosewater Cardamom Lassi is a filling, nourishing, soothing, and refreshing beverage. The peaches are delicious, and I used honey instead of sugar. Cardamom pairs well with peaches, which is surprising. Enjoy this as a dessert, a morning treat, a light meal on its own, or with your main course.

From an Ayurvedic Standpoint:

The popular Indian Lassi is given a western twist. Rosewater applies a sensual light touch to cooling yogurt, while peach warms it up. This tasty treat has depth and texture thanks to the light, aromatic cardamom. It's best if you use freshly ground cardamom.

Servings: 1

Time to Prepare: 10 minutes

Ingredients:

- ⅓ cup yogurt
- ½ whole peach
- ⅓ cup rose water
- ⅓ cup water
- 1 tsp honey
- 2 pinch cardamom
- A few pistachios for garnishing

Instructions:

1. Puree all ingredients in a blender.

2. Garnish with pistachios on top, if desired.

Coconut Water with Lime, Ginger, and Cardamom

Coconut Water with Lime, Ginger, and Cardamom is a unique, delicious, and energizing drink that is necessary to keep your body hydrated throughout the summer. It's a great drink to drink after a workout to replenish electrolytes. It's high in vitamins and nutrients, has a low sugar content, and is simple to make. It also serves well as a hunger quencher on hot summer days and as a way to replenish water during the harsh winter months.

From an Ayurvedic Standpoint:

This would be your favorite summer beverage because it is light, refreshing, and nutritious. It contains anti-inflammatory properties as well as electrolytes. Coconut water and coconut kernels can be beneficial in the treatment of diabetes. They have been shown to reduce pancreatic damage, increase insulin secretion, and improve blood glucose utilization. Diabetes, also known as Madhumeha, is caused by a Vata imbalance and poor digestion.

Servings: 1

Time to Prepare: 10 minutes

Ingredients:

- 1 cup coconut water
- ⅛-inch fresh ginger (minced or grated)
- ¼ tbsp lime
- ½ tsp sugar
- 2 pinch cardamom (powdered)

Instructions:

1. Blend all ingredients well and serve chilled.

INDIAN SPECIAL

Masala Poha (Spiced Flattened Rice)

Poha (Pohe) is a quick and easy Indian breakfast. Flattened rice, onions, spices, herbs, and peanuts are used to make this dish. This tasty and healthy dish is eaten in India, so there are various ways to prepare it. If you need a quick but tasty breakfast or snack but have little time, this is the recipe for you.

From an Ayurvedic Standpoint:

Poha is uncooked basmati rice that has been finely rolled, similar to how rolled oats are made. It cooks fast and requires no water other than what is absorbed during the washing process. Poha is simple to digest and beneficial to all three doshas. It is a healthy breakfast food or may be served as an accompaniment to the main course.

Servings: 4

Time to Prepare: 15 minutes

Ingredients:

- 3 cups Poha (the thick kind)
- ½ cup cilantro leaves (chopped)
- 1 small onion (chopped fine)
- 1 small green chili (chopped fine)
- 1 tomato (chopped)
- A handful of peanuts
- ⅓ cup sesame or sunflower oil
- 1 tsp black mustard seeds
- 1 tsp cumin seeds
- ½ tsp salt
- ½ tsp turmeric

- 1 pinch hing
- 5 curry leaves (fresh or dried)
- Lime and Sev (for garnishing)

Instructions:

1. Drain and set aside the rice flakes after washing them twice.

2. In a frying pan over medium heat, heat the oil and add the mustard seeds, cumin seeds, and curry leaves.

3. Stir in the turmeric, salt, and hing after the seeds have popped.

4. Add the cilantro, onions, peanuts, tomato, and chilli and cook until they're soft and slightly brown.

5. Stir in the rice flakes and mix well. Cover, and turn off the heat.

6. Allow to rest for a few minutes before serving, garnished with some additional cilantro, spicy sev, and a squeeze of fresh lime juice over each serving.

Quinoa Mung Dosa

Dosas are a form of vegan crepe or thin pancake that originated in southern India. It tastes amazing with Sambar and Coconut Chutney. While traditionally made with rice, this recipe uses quinoa due to the added benefits for Vata types.

From an Ayurvedic Standpoint:

Quinoa is a full protein that is particularly beneficial to Vata Dosha. This recipe is simple to prepare, and since it is light on the stomach, I recommend serving it as a dinner meal. Evening meals that are easily digested are beneficial to all doshas, but they are especially important for Vata. Mung Dal, on the other hand, is easy to digest and therefore gentle on the Agni, and its nourishing and grounding qualities make it ideal for both Vata and Kapha. The warming spices also help to balance Vata and Kapha, while igniting your Agni for more efficient digestion.

Servings: 5

Time to Prepare: 30 minutes

Ingredients:

- 1 cup organic whole green mung beans
- ½ tsp fresh ginger (finely grated)
- ½ cup organic quinoa
- 2 cups water
- ½ tsp cumin seeds
- ¼ tsp crushed black pepper

For filling:

- ¼ cup dry unsweetened coconut flakes
- 2 carrots (grated)
- 1 bunch cilantro (washed and chopped)
- ½ tsp salt

Instructions:

1. Soak the mung beans and quinoa together for at least 8 hours after washing thoroughly.

2. Drain the grains in the grinder/blender.

3. Add water little by little to achieve a fine consistency and a semi-liquid batter by grinding in between. (Remember to keep the cover on whenever you blend to prevent a mess)

4. Allow the batter to ferment for 2-3 hours.

5. After fermentation, mix cumin, pepper, ginger, and salt in it.

6. Heat the skillet over medium heat.

7. Coat the skillet with ½ tsp ghee or coconut oil.

8. Pour 2-3 tbsp of batter into the skillet and spread it out thinly like a pancake.

9. Cook for 1-2 minutes or until the bottom side is crisp and brown and the sides of the dosa start to unstick.

10. Next, bring the Dosa on a plate and top it with grated carrots, coconut, and cilantro.

12. Serve with Sambar and Coconut Chutney while still warm.

13. Proceed with the next Dosa in the same way.

Idli

Idli is a steamed savory cake made from rice and lentil batter (here I used mung dal instead of lentil for making this more Vata friendly). Each South Indian household makes Idli as a traditional breakfast. Idli is common not only in India but also internationally.

Idli is one of the healthiest breakfasts since it is naturally vegetarian, vegan, and gluten-free.

From an Ayurvedic Standpoint:

If allowed to ferment for long, idlis become sour and fermented, and hence Pitta provoking. Idlis may be astringent and drying for the colon depending on the dal used. Idlis can be tridoshic when served with Sambar and Mint Chutney.

It's also great for patients who have elevated cholesterol, high blood pressure, or heart problems. Calcium, iron, phosphorous, and magnesium are only a few of the essential minerals present in Idli that keep the body healthy and fit.

Servings: 4

Time to Prepare: 40 minutes

Ingredients:

- ¼ cup basmati rice
- ¼ cup mung bean
- 2 cups water
- ¼ tsp salt
- Ghee for coating ramekins

Instructions:

1. Soak rice and mung dal separately in different containers overnight with 1 cup of water each.

2. The next morning, strain the mung dal and add it to the rice and water. Blend until fully smooth.

3. Wait 2 days, or until bubbles form and the mixture smells fermented. (In warm climates, fermentation may be completed in as little as 8 hours.)

4. When fermented, add the salt and gently stir.

5. Coat the ramekins with ghee (we have separate Idli makers in India for steaming idlis, but otherwise pour batter into the ramekins).

6. Set aside for 20 minutes to allow the batter to rise slightly after pouring, resulting in lighter, fluffier idlis.

7. Steam for ten minutes, or until the mixture is light and fluffy.

8. Enjoy with Sambar and Coconut or Mint Chutney. (The Sambar recipe is listed below. You can also find the Coconut Chutney in the Chutney section.)

Sambar Chutney for Dosa and Idli

Sambar is a famous South Indian dish. Since it is produced from both lentils and vegetables, it is both balanced and nutritious. It is high in protein as well as other nutrients such as vitamins and minerals. Sambar is a complete meal when eaten with rice, dosa, or idli.

From an Ayurvedic Standpoint:

Sambar is tridoshic since it is well-balanced in terms of both flavors and ingredients, as well as including a strong combination of heating and cooling ingredients.

Replacing the toor dal with mung dal improves the digestibility of the sambhar without significantly altering the flavor. Mung dal is widely regarded as the most Sattvic of all lentils.

Vegetables may also be chosen depending on doshas. For example, grounding root vegetables such as carrots and potatoes can be beneficial to Vata. Lighter vegetables, such as zucchini, and leaves, such as spinach, can benefit Kaphas. Pittas can benefit from beans, bitter gourd, and leaves.

Servings: 3

Time to Prepare: 40 minutes

Ingredients:

For Sambhar Curry:

- 2 cups ash gourd/white pumpkin (cut into medium-sized cubes)
- ½ cup mung dal

- 2 potatoes (peel the skin and cut into large cubes)
- 2 carrots (cubed)
- 1 tomato (diced)
- 1 cup tamarind water
- 2 green chillies (split lengthwise)
- 1 drumstick (cut into 2-inch pieces)
- 10 shallots (cut into half)
- 1 tsp turmeric powder
- 1 sprig curry leaves
- 5 sprig coriander leaves (freshly chopped)
- Salt to taste

For homemade Sambhar powder:

- ½ cup fresh coconut (grated)
- 1 tsp black urad dal (Split)
- 1 tsp Bengal gram dal
- 1 tsp ghee or coconut oil
- 4 red chillies (dried)
- ¼ tsp fenugreek seeds
- 3 tsp coriander seeds
- ¼ tsp hing
- A few curry leaves

For seasoning:

- 2 tsp ghee or coconut oil
- ½ tsp mustard seeds
- 2 shallots (finely sliced, optional)
- 2 red chillies (dried)
- 1 sprig of curry leaves

Instructions:

1. First, we'll make the Homemade Roasted Coconut Sambar Powder.

2. In a heavy-bottomed pan, heat the ghee or oil and add the fenugreek seeds. Roast until lightly browned. Add in the broken urad dal and gram dal. Cook till they're golden brown.

3. Once the dals have turned brown, add the hing and fry for a few seconds, or until

the scent comes out. Transfer to a bowl and set aside to cool.

4. Roast the coriander seeds and dried red chillies in the same pan. Roast until they emit a pleasant fragrance and the red chillies are finely browned and roasted.

5. Stir in the curry leaves and grated coconut until the coconut browns (take care not to burn the coconut). Turn off the heat and set aside to cool.

6. Once cooled, add all the ingredients to a spice grinder and process until the dals and spices are grinding into a coarse powder-like texture. You can optionally add water to make a fine paste.

7. Once the powder is ready, proceed to the Sambar planning.

8. Add the tamarind water, turmeric powder, salt, and all the vegetables to a pressure cooker. Cook until you hear 2 whistles after adding a cup of water. Turn off the heat to allow the pressure to release spontaneously.

9. Add the lentils, cooked vegetables in tamarind water, and sambar powder in a large saucepan. To thoroughly mix all the ingredients, stir them together. Check the salt and spice levels, and adjust to taste. You may also thin out the sambar by adding water if you like it thinner.

10. Keep the heat to medium and simmer the Sambar for 5-6 minutes. While the Sambar is simmering, we'll prepare the seasoning.

11. In a small pan, heat the ghee or coconut oil; add the mustard seeds and allow them to crackle.

12. Add the thinly sliced pearl onions and cook until they soften and turn a light brown color.

13. Stir in the dried red chillies and curry leaves for a few seconds, or until the red chillies are roasted. This would take approximately 20 seconds.

14. Pour the seasoning over the simmering Sambar and top with sliced coriander leaves.

15. Turn off the heat and cover the Sambar for around 10-15 minutes before serving.

16. Serve this tasty Sambar with dosa, idli, uthappam, or vada.

Notes:
- Don't limit your use of veggies to those I have mentioned in the recipe.

You can add whichever vegetables are available in your refrigerator as per your Prakriti.

Chapati/Roti (Indian Flatbread)

A breakfast Chapati commonly eaten all across India is made with whole wheat flour in the shape of round circular shapes and served with any vegetable curry or side dish.

From an Ayurvedic Standpoint:

Wheat Chapati soothes Vata by providing warmth, heaviness, and softness. Cooked whole grain contains all these properties. Aside from its role in Vata balance, grain has a plethora of other beneficial properties. It is Sattvic in fact, which means it promotes balance and harmony.

Servings: 3

Time to Prepare: 40 minutes

Ingredients:

- 2 cups whole wheat flour
- 1 cup water
- 2 tbsp ghee (for mixing with dough)
- 3 tbsp ghee to apply all over the Chapatis
- Salt to taste

Instructions:

1. In a flat bottom vessel, add wheat flour, salt, and mix well.
2. Add little by little water at a time and knead the dough.
3. Knead the dough until it is soft.
4. At this stage, add the ghee, mix, and knead the dough into a very soft dough.
5. Cover and let the dough sit for 20 minutes.
6. Once the dough has rested well, press and knead it again.
7. Roll the dough with a rolling pin to soften it even further.
8. Once the dough appears soft, break it into medium-sized balls.

9. Dust the rolling board with some floor dust.

10. Place each dough ball on the board and flatten it into a round, circular disc-shaped Chapati.

11. Repeat with the remaining balls to make Chapatis.

To make the Chapati:

1. First, we make the phulka and then add the ghee.

2. Begin by placing the Chapati on the tawa.

3. Cook for a few seconds on the bottom side.

4. Flip and continue to cook the other side.

5. Extract the Chapati and place the half-cooked Chapati over the flame.

6. By puffing up, the half-cooked side is fully cooked.

7. Remove from the heat and serve immediately.

8. Brush all sides of the Roti with ghee or butter if desired.

9. Serve hot as a side dish with veg or non-veg curries.

Sabudana Vada

Sabudana Vada is a popular crisp fried snack made with tapioca pearls (Sago), roasted peanuts, boiled potatoes, and herbs. It is a common Maharashtrian snack that is eaten both as a tea-time snack and as a fasting or Upvas/Vrat meal.

From an Ayurvedic Standpoint:

Individuals with Vata Prakriti should consume a Vata-balancing diet that is moist, warm, and oily in nature. Sago (Sabudana) is an excellent addition to Vata's diet.

Servings: 12 vada

Time to Prepare: 30 minutes

Ingredients:

- 1½ cups soaked sago (sabudana)
- ¼ cup coriander (finely chopped)

- 1¼ cups potatoes (boiled, peeled, and mashed)
- ½ cup peanuts (roasted and coarsely crushed)
- 2 tsp green chilli paste
- 1 tsp grated ginger (grated)
- 1 tsp lemon juice
- Sesame oil for deep-frying
- 2 tsp sugar
- salt to taste

Instructions:

1. In a bowl, mix all the ingredients and thoroughly blend.

2. Divide the mixture into 12 equal portions and mold each into a 50 mm (2") diameter flat round. Keep aside.

3. Heat the oil in a pot and deep-fry the vadas on medium heat before they turn brown on both sides. Take out the vadas on an absorbent paper to soak excess oil. Then transfer them onto the plates.

4. Serve with fresh Cilantro Chutney or tomato sauce. (you will find the Cilantro Chutney recipe in the Chutney section.)

Notes:

- 1½ cup soaked sago = ½ cup raw sago washed, drained, and soaked in ¾ cup water for 4 to 5 hours, or until swollen and soft.

Pani Puri

Indian street food recipes are world famous because of the taste, flavor, and combination of spices. Most of them are either made with Ragda Curry or with the combination of deep-fried snacks in a Chaat Chutney. But there are some other unique water-based street food recipes and Pani Puri recipe or Golgappe is one such popular street food snack.

Ask any Indian, what is their favorite street food? Most will say Pani Puri! It is perhaps one of the most common and popular Indian street food recipes. Basically, it is a combination of street food recipes made with small Puri balls filled with spiced and mashed aloo and a specially made spiced water.

From an Ayurvedic Standpoint:

Sonth or Sunthi is Katu (pungent) in taste and Ushna (hot) in potency, making it an appetizer and digestive, according to Kaideva Nighantu (Ayurvedic medical text). It is also an aphrodisiac, treats respiratory disorders, cough, nausea and vomiting, hiccups, and constipation, and helps with Vata and Pitta Dosha imbalances. It is described in Rajanighantu as an appetizer and cardiac tonic. It is used to combat throat inflammation and diseases.

Cumin and tamarind, according to Ayurveda, help digestion, and cumin seeds are believed to balance all three doshas: Vata, Pitta, and Kapha. Herbs and spices used in preparing this soothing Ayurvedic energy drink have a calming impact on the body and help to restore one's appetite.

Dhauta Guda, or washed jaggery, cleanses the body of toxins and balances the Pitta Dosha. Ayurvedic practitioners, however, firmly advise utilizing old jaggery–at least one-year-old–to promote digestion, cleanse the gastrointestinal tract, urinary bladder, improve cardiac function, and combat anemia.

Chickpeas aid in the control of hyperpigmentation. It removes extra fat from the skin and leaves it with a lighter, more even complexion. It also aids in skin regeneration owing to its healing properties. And coriander seeds and cilantro are both digestive and cooling, balancing out some of the pungent and heating spices described earlier.

Servings: 4

Time to Prepare: 40 minutes

Ingredients:

For the Pani:

- 1 cup Sonth Chutney
- 2 cups mint leaves (firmly packed)
- 8 cups water
- 75 gm coriander leaves (ground together)
- 6-7 Green chillies
- 2 tbsp cumin seeds (roasted and powdered)
- 1 tbsp salt
- 1 tsp chilli powder
- A handful of coriander leaves (chopped)

For Sonth Ki Chutney:

- 100 gm tamarind (soaked in warm water for half an hour at least)
- ¾ cup jaggery (broken)
- ½ tsp garam masala
- 1 tsp dry ginger powder
- ¼ tsp black pepper powder
- ¼ tsp chilli powder
- 1 tsp chaat masala
- 2 tsp salt
- 1 tsp black rock salt

For Masala:

- 1½ cups potatoes (boiled, peeled, and mashed)
- ½ cup black chickpeas (boiled)
- 2 tbsp coriander Leaves (chopped)
- ½ tsp red chilli powder
- ½ tsp cumin powder
- ½ tsp coriander powder
- ¼ teaspoon chaat masala powder (available in any Indian grocery)
- Salt to taste

For Pani Puri:

- Pani of Pani Puri
- 24 puffed papdis
- Chickpea and potato masala

Instructions:

Preparing Pani:

1. Mix all the Pani ingredients and chill it for a while.

Preparing Sonth Ki Chutney:

1. Strain the tamarind through a strainer, using water to rinse.

2. Add just enough water to the pulp to make it pourable.

3. Stir in the remaining ingredients of Sonth Ki Chutney and bring to a boil, then reduce to low heat and let it simmer, stirring regularly until it thickens slightly.

4. Garnish with a handful of chopped coriander leaves.

Preparing masala:

1. In a mixing bowl, add the mashed potatoes, black chickpeas, red chilli powder, cumin powder, coriander powder, chaat masala, coriander leaves, and salt (add only if not already added when boiling the potatoes and chana).

2. Mix them with a spoon. Masala is done.

Preparing Pani Puri:

1. Make a hole in the center of the thinner side of the papdi, stuff it with masala, then fill it with Pani, and eat the whole Puri at once.

Bhel Puri

Bhel Puri is a delicious and flavorful Indian Chaat, easy to put together snack with the explosion of flavor and taste! It is a low-calorie snack that is addictive, tastes delicious, and is flavor-packed. Bhel Puri is most commonly sold by street vendors on the pushcarts in India. It is widely served in North Indian restaurants and Chaat centers. I recommend if you want to enjoy Indian flavors, Bhel Puri is a must-try!!

From an Ayurvedic Standpoint:

Bhel Puri is light on the stomach and super quick to bring together. There are several versions of this snack recipe, and every region adds its own mix of flavors to this authentic Indian recipe. The addition of various veggies, chutneys, and spices makes Bhel Puri suitable for all doshas.

Servings: 4

Time to Prepare: 30 minutes

Ingredients:

- 2 cups murmure (puffed rice)
- 15 crushed papdis (can be found in Indian grocery stores)
- ½ cup sev (can be found in Indian grocery stores)
- 2 large potatoes (boiled, peeled, and mashed)
- 2 large tomatoes (finely chopped)
- 1 large onion (finely chopped)

- 3 tbsp cilantro (finely chopped)
- 3 tbsp sweet and sour Tamarind Chutney (recipe in Chutney section)
- 2 tbsp Cilantro/Green Chutney (recipe in Chutney section)
- ½ tbsp lemon juice
- ½ tsp chilli powder
- ½ tsp chaat masala powder
- ½ tsp cumin powder
- Rock salt to taste

Instructions:

1. In a mixing bowl, add finely diced tomatoes, onions, and coriander leaves.

2. Stir in the boiled and mashed potatoes, as well as the puffed rice.

3. Stir in the tamarind and green chutney, cumin powder, chaat masala powder, lemon juice, and rock salt. Mix thoroughly.

4. When ready to serve, add crushed papdis and sev and mix well. Bhel Puri should be served right away.

Aloo Tikki Chaat

This tongue-satisfying Aloo Tikki Chaat recipe can take you to Indian street food. Tikki Chaat is a filling and appetizing snack that originated in North India but is now widely popular throughout India.

From an Ayurvedic Standpoint:

This tasty chaat recipe combines spicy, savory, sweet, sour, and creamy tastes and is perfect for all doshas on occasions.

Servings: 6

Time to Prepare: 30 minutes

Ingredients:

For Aloo Tikki:

- 5 medium potatoes (boiled and mashed)
- 3 tbsp cilantro (chopped)
- 3 tbsp rice flour

- 2 tbsp ghee
- ½ tsp ginger (finely chopped)
- ½ tsp green chillies (finely chopped)
- ½ tsp cayenne
- ½ tsp garam masala
- 1 tsp chaat masala
- Salt to taste

For Aloo Tikki Chaat:

- 1 cup thick yogurt
- 1 tbsp onions (chopped)
- 1 tbsp fine sev
- 2 tbsp green chutney
- 2 tsp sugar
- 1 tsp roast cumin powder
- 1 tsp black salt

Instructions:

1. Mash the potatoes and add chopped cilantro, cayenne, garam masala, chaat masala, chopped ginger-chilli, and salt. Blend thoroughly. Taste and adjust seasoning.

2. Mix in the rice flour thoroughly. Using your hands, shape patties, or Aloo Tikkis. Keep aside.

3. Warm up a skillet or tawa. Using 2 tbsp ghee or oil, shallow fry 5-6 Aloo Tikkis on both sides. Each side can take around 3-4 minutes. Continue to turn them until they are golden brown.

4. Your crispy, delicious Aloo Tikkis are now ready to eat. Cook the remaining Tikkis in the same way.

5. Serve these Tikkis plain or with Cilantro/Green Chutney or ketchup and a garnish of sliced onions.

Amritsari Chole

Amritsari Chole Masala is one of the best dishes in Punjabi cuisine. Amritsari Chole is also known as Chole Bhature because it is often served with a kind of fried bread named Naan. It is usually sold by street vendors, but it is also available in restaurants.

From an Ayurvedic Standpoint:

While this dish can be enjoyed by people of all doshas, the digestion-stimulating properties of garbanzo beans make it ideal for Vata people.

Servings: 4

Time to Prepare: 30 minutes

Ingredients:

For Cooked Chana:

- 1 cup dried kabuli chana/garbanzo beans (Soaked 5-6 hours or overnight)
- 1 whole black cardamom
- 1 bay leaf
- Salt to taste
- Pinch of baking soda
- Small piece of cinnamon stick
- 1 teabag (optional)

For Masala:

- 2 tbsp coriander seeds
- ½ tsp black peppercorns
- 1 tsp cumin seeds
- 1 tsp amchur powder (dried mango powder)
- 3 cloves
- Small piece of cinnamon
- 2 black cardamoms

For Gravy:

- 1 large onion (finely chopped)
- 2 tomatoes (finely chopped)
- 2 green chilli (roughly chopped)
- 1 tsp ginger (grated)
- 2 tbsp ghee
- 1 tsp red chilli powder
- 1 whole black cardamom
- 2 bay leaf
- Salt

Coriander leaves for garnishing

Instructions:

1. Pressure cook chickpeas within the required amount of water. Add baking soda, a tea bag, cinnamon, and one large black cardamom and pressure cook it for 10-12 minutes or till soft.

2. The chickpeas should be soft but not mushy. Discard the tea bag, drain the chana, and save the cooked chana water for later use.

3. Roast the dried masala ingredients in a pot for 3-4 minutes on low heat, then grind into a powder in a mixer/grinder and set aside.

4. In the same pot, heat the ghee. Sauté the green chillies, ginger, and bay leaf for a few seconds.

5. Sauté the sliced onion until it is transparent. Mix in the red chilli powder and salt.

6. Cook until the tomatoes are soft and the ghee has dispersed. Then stir in the prepared ground masala powder.

7. Add the cooked chana, mash some chana with a spatula, blend properly, and cook for 4-5 minutes on medium heat. Add the leftover water, salt, and if possible, another cup of water, and bring to a boil for 7-8 minutes, or until the gravy thickens.

8. Garnish with fresh coriander leaves if desired. Serve warm with bhatura, naan, or rotis.

Butter Naan

Beside Chole, every Indian craves soft, delicious Butter Naan made with all-purpose flour. It is a leavened bread that is extremely common in South Asia. In India, this is one bread that is always on the menu of any party, wedding, and birthday celebration. You can make Naan on an iron tawa by flipping it upside down, or you can cook Naan in a tandoor or cooker by sticking it sideways.

From an Ayurvedic Standpoint:

While this is not something one should consume daily, it's a heavy food. And that's the reason why in India people don't eat it daily, although it is extremely delicious. But in moderation, this can be consumed by all doshas.

Servings: 11-12 naans

Time to Prepare: 30 minutes

Ingredients:

- 4 cup all-purpose flour (maida)
- ½ cup curd or yogurt (fresh and thick)
- 4 tbsp oil
- 4 tbsp butter/ghee
- 2 tbsp sugar
- 2 tbsp baking powder
- ½ tbsp baking soda
- salt to taste
- Lukewarm water (as required)

Instructions:

1. In a mixing bowl, combine maida, sugar, baking powder, baking soda, salt, curd, oil, and blend well. Knead the dough for 10 minutes with lukewarm water and then grease with a few drops of ghee or oil.

2. Cover with a wet cloth and set aside in a warm place for 1-2 hours.

3. After 2 hours, knead the dough lightly with a few drops of oil to eliminate any air.

4. Shape the dough into balls.

5. Using a rolling pin, gently roll the dough into circular shapes. Be sure not to make it too thin or too thick, just have the size in mind. It should not be bigger than the size of your tawa.

6. Brush the Naan with water.

7. Finally, gently turn it over and place it on a hot tawa with water on one side of the Naan and slightly press it so it sticks to the tawa.

8. After a minute, a few bubbles can be seen on Naan.

9. Flip the tawa upside down and cook the Naan directly on the flame until golden brown. Make sure it bakes evenly on both sides, but don't let it burn.

10. Loosen the Naan by gently scraping it from the bottom.

11. Brush with butter/ghee. Finally, serve the warm Butter Naan with your favorite

curries, such as Shahi Paneer or Chole.

Makki Di Roti Te Sarson Da Saag (Corn Flour Flat Bread and Mustard Greens)

The is a classic Punjabi dish best served with some white butter, jaggery, and Chatti Di Lassi. This delicious and nutrient-rich combination is prepared during the winters, especially on the occasion of the festival of Lohri.

From an Ayurvedic Standpoint:

Due to its heating properties, Sarson Da Saag is associated with cold, wet winter months. Its main ingredient mustard greens are tender, bitter, heating making it great green to enjoy during Kapha season but not so great for Vata and Pitta. But when mixed with ghee, which is cooling and moist, helps to balance the heat, bitter, and dry properties of the greens (especially if you have a Vata imbalance or are Vata dominant).

Servings: 3

Time to Prepare: 50 minutes

Makki Di Roti (Corn Flour Flat Bread)

Ingredients:

- 2 cups of yellow corn flour
- Ghee
- Salt to taste
- Some warm water

Instructions:

1. Knead the flour of the corn with a little salt and warm water.

2. Create the balls out of the dough.

3. Pat the balls with the palm of your hand to produce rotis (flatbread).

4. Use a butter paper as your board.

5. Get the roti slightly thicker than the normal roti.

6. Move the roti to a hot pan and cook on low heat; switch to the other side until both sides are toasted.

7. To intensify the flavor, add some ghee. Serve with Sarson Da Saag.

Sarson Da Saag (Mustard Greens)

Ingredients:

- ¼ kg of spinach (finely chopped)
- 2 tbsp. corn flour (sieved)
- 1 kg of mustard greens (finely chopped)
- A small piece of ginger (minced)
- 2 green chillies (minced)
- 2 red chillies
- Ghee (or vegan ghee)
- Salt to taste

Instructions:

1. Add the greens of mustard and spinach until soft.

2. Add a pinch of salt and chopped green chilli pepper while cooking.

3. Extract the excess water and mix the leafy vegetables well. Set it back.

4. Heat the ghee and add the ginger, the green chillies, and the broken red chillies until they become slightly brown.

5. Add a little salt to the mashed greens and stir.

6. Mix the corn flour in a little water and add it to the mixture.

7. Allow boiling for about 30 minutes.

8. Serve hot with Makki Di Roti.

Jaljeera

Jaljeera, also known as Jal Jeera, is a healthy, refreshing Indian summer drink. As part of a North Indian style thali, this spiced minty summer cooler is consumed as an appetizer drink (lunch). The aroma and taste of fresh mint and coriander leaves are energizing.

From an Ayurvedic Standpoint:

Jaljeera not only satisfies thirst but also stimulates appetite and helps digestion. Jal jeera simply means "cumin water," but this drink is far more than roasted cumin seeds.

Cumin and tamarind, according to Ayurveda, help digestion, and cumin seeds are believed to balance all three doshas—Vata, Pitta, and Kapha. Herbs and spices used in preparing this soothing Ayurvedic energy drink have a calming impact on the body and help to restore one's appetite.

Servings: 5

Time to Prepare: 25 minutes

Ingredients:

- ⅓ cup fresh mint leaves (washed and chopped roughly)
- A lemon-sized tamarind ball soaked in warm water for 10 minutes
- 2 tbsp sugar dissolved in ¼ cup water
- ½ cup fresh coriander leaves (washed and chopped roughly)
- 1 tsp ginger (grated)
- 1 tbsp lemon juice (optional)
- 1 cup tap water
- 4 cups cold water
- Boondi (for garnish)

For Jaljeera powder:

- ½ tsp dry mango powder
- ¼ tsp hing
- ¾ tbsp cumin seeds
- ½ tsp black peppercorns
- 2 cloves
- 1 black cardamom
- 1 tsp black salt
- ½ tsp rock salt
- ¼ tsp fennel seeds (optional)

Instructions:

1. Dry roast cumin seeds for 5-6 minutes on low to medium heat. Remove the pan

from the heat and put it aside.

2. After that, dry roast the fennel seeds for 3 minutes and put them aside. Then dry roast the cloves, black cardamom, and black peppercorns for 2 minutes and put them aside.

3. Grind the spices, along with black salt, rock salt, dry mango powder, and hing, to a fine powder once they've cooled.

4. To make a fine paste, add the coriander leaves, mint leaves, and ginger with a cup of water. Pour the ground paste into a strainer and set aside the strained juice.

5. Add a liter of cold water into the strained juice. Stir in the tamarind extract, sugar water, and lemon juice.

6. Add 2 tbsp ground Jaljeera powder to the liquid and mix completely. Add more water if the Jaljeera is too tangy. Lemon juice may be added if it requires more tang. Taste and adjust seasonings as required, then chill until ready to serve.

7. Pour into large containers when ready to serve. Garnish with boondi and ice cubes.

Notes:

- Jaljeera can be stored in the refrigerator for a few days.
- The ground Jaljeera powder can be kept in an airtight container. It can be kept for up to 4-5 months.
- Add a slit green chilli to the Jaljeera for added spice.
- You can also use honey or jaggery syrup in place of sugar.

Masala Chai (Masala Tea)

Masala Chai can undoubtedly be designated as India's National Drink! Many Indians like to have a cup of tea in the morning or the evening. Most Indians get a headache if they don't drink their daily cup of tea.

Many herbs and spices are added to tea in India. Every family has its own way of producing tea. When you don't have masala tea powder, this recipe will show you how to make Masala Chai. Just a few whole spices are needed. It tastes fantastic and takes about 10 minutes to prepare.

From an Ayurvedic Standpoint:

Fall season has the potential to aggravate Vata Dosha. The spices in this Masala Chai are warming and satisfying to Vata Dosha. The milk adds a fatty, heavy, grounding quality. Because of their sweet and spicy flavors, ginger, cardamom, and cinnamon are especially balancing to Vata. Cloves are suitable for Vata, but since they are pungent (meaning hot and/or purifying), it is better not to overdo them.

Servings: 3

Time to Prepare: 11 minutes

Ingredients:

- 2 cups/500 ml milk
- ¼ cup water
- 2 tsp Assam or Darjeeling Tea
- 1 tsp fennel seeds
- 4 tsp sugar (or more as per taste)

For masala:

- 1-inch ginger
- ½-inch cinnamon
- 2 cloves
- 2-3 green cardamoms

Instructions:

1. Take cinnamon, cardamoms, fennel seeds, cloves, and ginger in a mortar-pestle. Crush coarsely and keep aside.

2. In a saucepan or small pan, heat the water. Let the water come to a boil and then add the crushed spices.

3. Boil the spices along with the water for a minute.

4. Add sugar as per taste (I usually add 4 tsp raw sugar). You can add more or less as per your choice.

5. Now add the tea. Boil for a minute. (This boiling time depends on how strong you want your tea. If you prefer a strong tea, boil for a few more minutes.)

6. Add milk. After adding milk, boil for 5-7 minutes.

7. If using chilled milk, then boil with tea for 2-3 minutes. If using hot milk, then add the milk and switch off the flame.

8. Pour the tea through a tea strainer directly into the cup. Enjoy this Masala Chai with some cookies or Indian biscuits!

FOOD COMBINING FOR DOSHAS

Those were just a few recipes you can have to pacify your Vata Dosha, but don't let it restrict you from trying something new. You can always experiment with your meal as per your Prakriti. Just keep one thing in mind, avoid combining foods that are not compatible together. The guidelines of food combining are a must to keep in mind for anyone who wants to care for his/her doshic health.
The Ayurvedic viewpoint on food combination is incredibly fascinating—and for many people, it acts as a launchpad to understanding more about Ayurveda's ancient wisdom teachings!

Many people are unfamiliar with the idea of food combining—the theory that certain foods digest well together and others do not. However, it is a vital aspect of learning how to eat properly, according to Ayurveda, much as knowing one's constitution and condition of imbalance is important for Ayurvedic self-discovery.

Careful food combining will significantly increase digestion, assist the body in receiving deeper nourishment, and have a beneficial effect on our overall well-being. Most people in the western world, though, are used to consuming a variety of items that do not naturally digest well together (like fruit with nuts, or beans with cheese).

So, what's the point? According to the Ayurvedic perspective on diet, each food has a unique mix of tastes and energies, as well as a corresponding impact on both the digestive system and the body as a whole. Since food is such an important catalyst for well-being and making changes in your well-being, Ayurveda suggests tailoring your diet to the dosha you are seeking to achieve.

Each of the three doshas has its own effect on digestion. Vata induces irregular digestion, which means that it may be amazing at times but often cause gas and bloating. Pitta is used to aid digestion. Most foods are fine for persons with decent Pitta, although acidic and spicy foods can induce heartburn and digestive distress. Kapha, on the other hand, is the slowest of the three to digest.

Every food has its own flavor (Rasa), a heating or cooling energy (Virya), and a post-digestive effect (Vipaka), according to Ayurveda. Some people also have Prabhava, an unknown effect.

According to Ayurveda, our gut health is a determinant of our overall health, and it is critical to learn how to keep our Agni, or digestive fire, powerful and effective. Our Agni is a large soup of acid, bile, and enzymes that aid in the conversion of food into useful energy. Maintaining a healthy Agni results in improved absorption, elimination, and immune function.

But although an individual's Agni plays a role in how well or poorly food is digested, food combinations are also important. When two or more foods with contrasting flavors, energies, and post-digestive effects are mixed, Agni may become overwhelmed, inhibiting the enzyme mechanism and resulting in the production of toxins. However, if eaten separately, these same foods can stimulate Agni, be digested more quickly, and even aid in the burning of Ama.

Combining foods with vastly different energetics will overburden the digestive fire (Agni), resulting in indigestion, fermentation, gas, bloating, putrefaction, and toxin production, which, if left unchecked, will contribute to toxaemia and disease. Eating bananas with milk, for example, will reduce Agni, alter intestinal flora, create toxins, and induce sinus infection, cold, cough, and allergies. While both of these foods have a sweet flavor and cooling energy, their post-digestive effects are somewhat different - bananas are sour, whereas milk is sweet. This confuses our digestive tract and may contribute to toxins, allergies, and other imbalances.

This is why proper food combination is important.

Of course, certain combinations are more likely to upset the digestive system than others, which is a vital fact if you are new to this practice. Giving attention to how you mix ingredients, regardless of any specific preferences or effects, will offer a valuable opportunity for understanding, healing, and better health.

There are optimal food options that you can use based on your dosha and season to promote equilibrium in your mind and body. The chart below, on the other hand, maybe used for all doshas.

The collection below illustrates contradictory foods and suggests more suitable combinations. It is intended to be a reference, not a comprehensive list. In fact, you may be aware of other combinations that are harmful to your body.

Foods	**Compatible**	**Incompatible**

Beans	Grains, vegetables, other beans, nuts, seeds	Fruit, milk, cheese, yogurt, eggs, meat, fish
Butter and Ghee	Grains, vegetables, beans, nuts, seeds, cooked fruit	Ghee combines better than butter with most food because it's cooked longer
Cheese	Grains, vegetables	Fruit, beans, eggs, milk, yogurt, hot drinks
Milk	Best alone. Exceptions: rice pudding, oatmeal, dates, almonds	Any other food (especially bananas, cherries, melons, sour fruits, yeasted bread, eggs, yogurt, meat, fish, khichdi, starches)
Yogurt	Grains, vegetables	Fruit, beans, milk, cheese, eggs, meat, fish, nightshades, hot drinks
Fruit	Other fruits with similar qualities, (i.e., citrus together, apples and pears, a berry medley)	Any other food (aside from other fruit) except dates with milk, and some cooked combinations
Lemons	Usually okay with other foods if used in small amounts	Cucumbers, tomatoes, milk, yogurt. Note: lime can be substituted for use with cucumbers and tomatoes
Melons	Best to have each type of melon alone	Everything (especially dairy, eggs,

		fried food, grains, starches
Grains	Beans, vegetables, other grains, nuts, seeds, cheese, yogurt	Fruit
Vegetables	Grains, beans, other vegetables, cheese, yogurt, nuts, seeds	Fruit, milk
Nightshades (peppers, eggplant, potatoes, tomatoes)	Other vegetables, grains, beans, meat, fish, nuts, seeds	Fruit (especially melon), cucumber, milk, cheese, yogurt
Hot drinks	Most foods, unless the hot drink contains other foods (i.e., milk, fruit) in which case reference that particular food	Mangoes, cheese, yogurt, meat, fish, starches
Leftovers	Ideally, just other leftovers from the same meal. Preferably not over 24 hours old.	Freshly cooked foods
Raw foods	Other raw foods	Cooked foods (especially in large quantities)

Ayurveda, like a proper food combination, is intended to be intuitive. However, if your present diet and lifestyle have overruled your intuition, it may take some time to get into a new rhythm that is more as per your true nature. Thus, start small. Maybe something on the food chart sticks out to you, something you eat daily. If so, start there. Otherwise, try printing the chart and sticking it on your refrigerator; let it soak in your subconscious and have a look at it before you cook a lunch or grab a snack.

VATA SEASONAL GUIDE (RITUCHARYA)

Each season is identified with a dosha in Ayurveda—Spring with Kapha, Summer with Pitta, and Autumn and Winter with Vata. Each of these doshas has a propensity to increase with the metabolism during its season. Thus, the heat of summer tends to make Pitta worse in us, while dry, cold, and windy winters tend to increase Vata.

Such seasonal variations of the doshas within us can be controlled by feeding well for the season. Desh (place) and Kala (time) are important considerations when it comes to choosing what you eat.

If you enquire, some of these choices come naturally to most of us—like we're heading for cool drinks on a hot day, and we're eager to wrap our fingers around a steaming cup of soup on a chilly evening.

Vata Dosha is composed of elements of air and space, and it governs all movement within the body. Vata is the dominant seasonal dosha between mid-October and mid-February. Even for those with fewer Vata, it is important to take steps to keep Vata in check during this period because of its seasonal impact.

Signs of exacerbated Vata include abnormal vomiting, indigestion, nausea, constipation, intestinal cramping, slow assimilation, and fatigue.

So, how to reduce Vata Dosha with diet in winter is the key to maintaining healthy immunity in winter. The two key elements of the Vata-pacifying diet are warm and cooked foods.

For starters, warm soups and stews, hot cereals, and hot drinks such as herb teas are perfect for preserving your body's temperature and, in effect, your immunity. The predominant tastes are sweet, sour, salty, bitter, pungent, and astringent.

Sweet, sour, and dense fruits such as oranges, bananas, cherries, pineapples, berries, and cooked vegetables such as beets, cabbage, asparagus, and sweet potatoes are the best food to be eaten in the winter.

Some of Vata's herbs and spices are cardamom, cumin, oregano, cloves, and turmeric. There are many questions, such as how to keep the body warm naturally and how to reduce Vata in the body in the winter. A simple solution to achieve this is to maintain a strict diet for your food and to eat it at regular and proper intervals.

It's important not to skip any meals, to have a heavy breakfast and lunch, and to have a lighter dinner. Also, remember to have dinner at least 3 hours before you go to bed. You can eat nuts and raisins soaked in water to satisfy your hunger pangs in-between meals.

Here is how you can keep your Vata in check during the winter:

Choose Warm over Cold

Cooked foods, served hot, are perfect for you to consume. Hearty soups, warm cereals, rice pudding, and wholesome beverages such as nut milk or warm milk are excellent 'comfort' foods for you.

Foods with a cooling base, such as cold and frozen food or carbonated drinks, raw food, and refrigerated leftovers will make Vata worse even if served warm.

Warm quality can be emphasized by eating foods that are warm at temperatures, and by generously using warm spices. Vata-pacifying spices include cardamom, cumin, ginger, cinnamon, salt, cloves, mustard seed, and moderately black pepper.

"Warm" and "cooked" are key factors in the Vata-pacifying diet. Nourishing soups, broths, and stews are all welcome on cold winter days. Steamed food is a good option for winter wellness and nutrition.

Choose Moist and Oily over Dry

Balance the dry quality of Vata with "heavy" foods such as oils and ghee. Always drink plenty of hydrating drinks, soups, and stews—either served hot or moderately warm, no colder than room temperature.

Moist foods such as berries, melons, summer squash, zucchini, and yogurt will counter Vata's dryness. Oily foods may account for this dosha and favor foods such as avocado, coconut, olives, buttermilk, cheese, whole milk (preferably non-homogenized), wheat, nuts, and seeds.

If you are of this type, stop drying foods such as popcorn, crackers, white potatoes, beans, and dried fruit. Vata's dryness is reduced by eating cooked food rather than raw food. By cooking and garnishing food with ample amounts of ghee and keeping it hydrated, you can reduce Vata dryness.

Choose Wholesome, Nourishing, and Soothing over Light

Although heaviness is a perfect way to counteract Vata's lightness, avoid deep-fried foods that can burden your fragile digestion.

It's also important that you don't overeat because taking too much food in one sitting can be too heavy. Such foods are typically sweet to taste like cooked grains, spiced milk, root vegetables, stewed fruit, nuts, and seeds. You can stay away from canned foods, ready-to-eat dinners, and pastries that can be too hard to handle. Likewise, Vata-dominant people should stay away from caffeine, nicotine, and alcohol as they are hazardous to your need to remain balanced and stable.

Choose Smooth over Rough

Raw produce is called roughage for good reason, and Vatas will do well to note that. The rough consistency of these foods will only threaten the digestive capability of this dosha.

In fact, you will benefit from resisting cooked foods with rough textures such as broccoli, cabbage, cauliflower, leafy greens, and certain types of beans.

Smooth foods such as bananas, rice pudding, warm cereal, hot spiced milk, and soups soothe Vata's roughness.

AYURVEDIC DIET FAQS

1. Do Vata Dosha and Fasting Go Well?

Fasting is not most of the time suitable for Vata types. But if you really want to do a fast, Ayurveda recommends fasting only once a week for no more than 4 weeks. 12–24-hour fast is a good place to start.

And if you do it in the spring, that's even better because the weather is getting warmer. Have broth or other moist soupy beverages for all three meals during that day. You can mono-fast with sweet orange, mango, or grape juice, all of which are Vata pacifying. You're never supposed to go without any food.

2. Do Vata Dosha and Warm Foods Go Well?

Warm food usually refers to the temperature of the food. In Ayurveda, however, we are also talking about the heating of spices or foods with heating properties. Both are generally good at pacifying Vata.

The advantage of these hot spices is that you can prepare food that is Vata aggravating with heating and grounding spices such as ginger and garlic. You can cook beans so that they don't make Vata worse than it was at the beginning.

On the other hand, it is best to avoid products with cooling properties and foods taken directly from the refrigerator, such as cold drinks. Even pre-cooked, refrigerated foods that are heated in a microwave or otherwise lacking in the quality of Prana or life essence. They are not recommended as well.

Freshly cooked foods are always preferred. Oily and moist foods are beneficial in Vata pacification. The warm nature can be enhanced by eating foods that are both energetically warming and warm at temperature, and by the liberal use of digestive spices.

On the other hand, it is possible to avoid energy-cooling foods, such as chilled and frozen food or drinks, carbonated drinks, large quantities of raw fruits and vegetables, and even leftovers stored in the refrigerator or freezer.

The cold quality of these foods is naturally increases, so it is safer to cook freshly. But again, you have to be practical about what you can do, and the leftover mung dal is going to be much more Vata-pacifying than canned black bean soup or raw kale salad.

3. Where and When to Eat?

Besides being mindful of vegetarian diet, food combinations, and the 6 tastes, aim to bear the following in mind:

Do you feed at the same time and place every day? The Ayurvedic tradition includes feeding only when you are hungry, as well as not eating after 7 p.m., in between meals, even when you are irritated or angry. It's also necessary to sit when eating (but not in your car) and pay attention to what you're eating (the taste, texture, smell of the food). For example, don't watch TV or use any other electronic device during meals.

Ayurveda advises developing a calm eating atmosphere while preventing heated debates or disputes as much as possible.

4. What's a Balanced Meal?

The quantity and kind of food you consume have a huge impact on your health and well-being. According to Ayurveda, try to keep the amount of food you eat during each meal equivalent to two cupped handfuls.

It is also recommended that you keep your meals nutritious and limit items that are too heavy and dense. Furthermore, Ayurveda suggests you eat a range of foods and that you consume each food in moderation. It is therefore important to avoid excluding entire food groups, such as a no-fat or no-carb diet. Remember to chew your food thoroughly before swallowing, and to take sips of warm water (but not too much) during your meal to facilitate digestion.

5. Why Your Body Type Matter?

The leading eating principles are determined by one's body type. The universe is made up of 5 components, according to Ayurveda: Vayu (air), Jala (water), Akash (space), Teja (fire), and Prithvi (earth). These components are thought to combine to create three distinct doshas, or body types, which correspond to the energy that circulates inside the body. Although everybody has traits from all three doshas, one is usually dominant:

Vata (air and space) governs fundamental bodily processes such as the mind, breathing, blood supply, and digestion. This dosha is characterized by slimness and energy. When they are out of balance, they may suffer from stomach problems, fatigue, weight loss, insomnia, or anxiety.

Pitta (fire and water) governs metabolism, hormones, and digestion. People with a Pitta Dosha are usually of medium build. If they are out of balance, they can suffer from elevated blood pressure, heart failure, inflammation, or digestive issues.

Kapha (water and earth) governs immunity, muscle development, and power. Many with a Kapha Dosha have a more robust frame. They may have issues with weight control, fluid absorption, diabetes, depression, allergies, or respiratory health if they are out of balance.

The dosha decides which things you should consume and which you should avoid. And, according to Ayurvedic practice, once you are in balance, you would instinctively crave foods that are most essential for your optimum health.

6. What's the Right Way of Cooking?

It is necessary to be in a happy state of mind while cooking, according to Ayurveda. This is because the feelings you put into your food when cooking can affect those that consume it, so make sure you put a lot of love into anything you prepare.

When cooking, attempt to make the experience as settled and conscious as possible, rather than throwing everything together under stress. Allow yourself time to relax and appreciate the simple process of cooking, tasting the ingredients, enjoying the textures, and having fun.

Last but not least, food should be a pleasurable experience. After all, you're nourishing your mind, body, and soul.

7. What are the Health Benefits of an Ayurvedic Diet?

Eating according to your dosha and having a spiritual connection with food can result in healthy digestion, immunity, bowel movements, and energy. According to Ayurveda, if the stomach and digestion are healthy, anything else would be well.

While the ultimate aim of eating according to your dosha is to achieve good health and wellness, you will notice other benefits too. Since the Ayurvedic Diet discourages the consumption of processed foods, it can assist you in reducing your consumption of saturated fats, added sugar, and sodium—ingredients that are commonly found in highly processed foods and have been related to cardiac disease, obesity, and high blood pressure, according to the Harvard School of Public Health.

Plus, Ayurveda doesn't just look at the food texture or taste but also at the Prakriti of the food. It classifies food on their specific energetics—Sattvic, Rajasic, and Tamasic. Ayurveda recommends Sattvic food because it has the most positive energetics and as you may know, we're what we eat. If you eat foods that have positive energetics, you'll be filled with positivity.

On the other hand, if you eat Rajasic or Tamasic foods, especially Tamasic foods that have negative energetics, then you're filling yourself with negative energies. (Tamasic foods include meats and it's obvious that when a being is killed there are negative emotions in the body which after death remains. And when we consume them, we're filled with those negative emotions of fear, anger, agony, etc.)

8. Can the Ayurvedic Diet Lead to Weight Loss?

Although little research on the effects of an Ayurvedic Diet has been reported, there are some positive outcomes. In one small study that combined the diet with other Ayurvedic health activities such as meditation and stress management, participants lost a total of 13 pounds over 9 months.

Overall, the diet emphasizes whole foods while minimizing refined foods, a trend that increases nutrient, mineral, protein, and antioxidant intake and can aid in weight control. According to one report, switching from packaged to whole foods without reducing calorie consumption resulted in an approximately 50% rise in post-meal calorie burning.

Ayurvedic Diets also have a lot of herbs and spices. Some natural seasonings, besides being high in antioxidants, often function as prebiotics, nourishing the protective intestinal bacteria linked to anti-inflammation, immunity, and a happy mood. Herbs and spices have been found to increase satiety. Some, such as ginger and hot peppers, are believed to boost metabolism.

AUTHOR NOTE

So, I think I've been able to provide you a deeper insight on Ayurvedic Cooking for Vata Dosha. Thank you for reading one of my books! This is the 25th book I've written since 2018. It took me a long time to write my first book, mostly because I was new to the writing world and has very little knowledge of how to publish books.

I thought my first book will be a Bestseller, but as you may guess it didn't go well, in fact, I got a negative review on it by the 3rd reader itself.

I learned a lot over time and still learning something new every day. And as I am on this journey, I realized that writing books is a great way to reach people around the world and share some valuable knowledge.

Moreover, I enjoy writing books, books that can help people to be content, happy, and healthy in all aspects of well-being (Mind, Body, and Soul). It may sound idiotic, but I've left my full-time job just to write books more efficiently.

Why am I telling you all this?? Because I think it's important that readers should know their value. You can give your review on books, trust me that's a superpower!

Not just authors, but you too add value to a book. Referring to your reviews, a reader decides whether or not to invest in that book. You can make or break the journey of a book, that's your power!

Your review is extremely valuable to me; I really want to know what you think of my books. No, I'm not manipulating you to give me a 5-star review, you're free to judge. Just don't go without leaving a review!

It'll help others get a better idea of the book. For me, it'll motivate me towards writing and improving more.

So please share your meaningful review of this book! Here's a link that'll take you directly to the review section- Click Here

Once again thanks for reading...

You can lend this book to your family, it's free of cost!!

You can contact me for any queries: rohit@rohitsahu.net or on any of the following social media:

Facebook, Twitter, Instagram, Goodreads, Linkedin: Rohit Sahu

Of course, Eating as per Ayurvedic Dietary Guidelines can Help a Lot in Balancing Your Dosha, But that's Just One Aspect alongside Other Ayurvedic Practices, Physical Exercises, and Lifestyle. To Learn All that Aspects about Each Dosha, Check Out this Ayurveda For Beginners Series:

In each book, we'll dive deeper into what that's specific dosha means, what throws it out of balance, and how to identify the dosha in your environment, in yourself, and in others.

With these books, I've shared with you everything you need to know to balance the doshas and use them to your overall vitality, joy, and well-being.

Just follow these books along, and you'll reveal the easiest step-by-step routine to balance your specific dosha by the end of it!

They're available in every online bookstore...

HERE'S YOUR FREE GIFT!!

CHAKRAS FOR BEGINNERS
A Guide to Understanding 7 Chakras of the Body

Nourish, Heal, And Fuel The Chakras For Higher Consciousness And Awakening!

ROHIT SAHU

If you're into chakras and pursuing knowledge about Chakras Awakening and Vibrational Energy, this book will help you pave the way towards your spiritual growth. You can also join the mailing list to be the first to hear new release updates, improved recommendations, and bonus contents.

Being on my email list means you'll be the first to know when I release a new book. I plan to release them at a steep discount (or even FREE) for the first 24 hours.

By signing up for my list, you'll get early notifications. And if you don't want to join my list, it's totally fine. It just means that I just need to earn your trust.

Click Here to Claim Your Free Book!!
or follow this link- https://bit.ly/chakrasforbeginners

Click Here to Join My Mailing List

or follow this link if this is a paperback- http://bit.ly/theMailingList

MORE FROM AUTHOR

» Ayurveda Cookbook For Beginners- Pitta

» Ayurveda Cookbook For Beginners- Kapha

» Ayurveda For Beginners- Vata

» Ayurveda For Beginners- Pitta

» Ayurveda For Beginners- Kapha

» Yoga For Beginners (Series)

» Step-By-Step Beginners Instant Pot Cookbook (Vegan): 100+ Easy, Delicious Yet Extremely Healthy Instant Pot Recipes Backed By Ayurveda Which Anyone Can Make In Less Than 30 Minutes

» Spiritual Empath: The Ultimate Guide To Awake Your Maximum Capacity To Have That Power, Compassion, And Wisdom Contained In Your Soul

» Who Are You: The Spiritual Awakening Self Discovery Guide For Enlightenment And Liberation

» Chakras for Beginners: A Guide to Understanding 7 Chakras of the Body: Nourish, Heal, And Fuel The Chakras For Higher Consciousness And Awakening! (Available for FREE!!)

» Shadow Work For Beginners: A Short and Powerful Guide to Make Peace with Your Hidden Dark Side that Drive You and Illuminate the Hidden Power of Your True Self for Freedom and Lasting Happiness